"There are some books that, in God's providence, are written by exactly the right person and come along at just the right time to forward God's redemptive mission in this world. *Church for Monday: Equipping Believers for Mission at Work* by Dr. Svetlana Papazov fits that description perfectly. With the first-hand insight of a practitioner and the visionary lens of a spiritual entrepreneur, Dr. Papazov shows us that reaching the 8-to-5 workday window (where most unchurched people spend the majority of their waking hours) is both essential and doable. The result: an embedded Church that integrates faith into the real-world environments of ordinary people with whole-life transformation as the outcome. Now, that gets my blood pumping! Church for Monday is a breakthrough book for ministry leaders willing to take innovative risks to reach their communities, and a must-read for anyone who longs to see the Good News reach beyond Sunday Church into a waiting, 7-day-a-week world."

– **Dr. Jodi Detrick**, Author of *The Jesus-Hearted Woman: 10 Leadership Qualities for Enduring & Endearing Influence*

"It is quite rare for visionaries and leaders to demonstrate also a "well-lived theology." With refreshing perspective and authenticity that only come by a wealth of experience, Dr. Svetlana Papazov offers in this work a most useful resource, wedding sound ecclesiological commitment and very practical strategies for being the *Church for Monday*. Beyond any status quo wineskin, Svetlana communicates a Gospel priority for the generation of image-bearers who have been marginalized and disenfranchised. This book represents the potential to change radically our communities across the nation."

– **Dr. Kevin Dudley**, Assistant Professor of Church and Society, Trinity Lutheran Seminary, Columbus, OH

"The Sunday-to-Monday movement in our churches is gaining steam, and Dr. Svetlana Papazov has been a blessing to our movement for years. It's great to see her insights written down so their catalytic impact can reach further. If you're thinking about how

to connect Sunday to Monday, you'll find a lot of stimulating ideas here."
    – **Greg Forster**, Ph.D., Director, Oikonomia Network

"A book to unshackle the confines of a faith experienced and expressed only inside a religious building or in private solitude. Dr. Papazov's vision expands the experience of a Christian faith to be what it was meant to be, lived from the inside out, 24/7, and positively impacting others. Accept the challenge to at least think about flourishing at a whole new level and in a new way, for it is, indeed Christ's call to be a *Church for Monday*."
    – **Dr. Timothy A. Hager**, Vice President, Evangel University and Dean, Assemblies of God Theological Seminary, Springfield, MO

"Well done. So comprehensive. A desperately needed call to reformat the Church as it now is to make tangible, missionally effective moves toward the Church it must be to reach the post, perhaps pre-, Christian culture in which we now live. I believe God is going to use Dr. Svetlana Papazov's work as a part of His plan to save the mission of His Church in America."
    – **Steve Pike**, Founder, Church Multiplication Network, President, Urban Islands Project, Author of Total Fitness for Your Church, and Co-Author of *Leading Church Multiplication*

"*Church for Monday* is for everyone! Dr. Papazov has pastorally, intellectually, and creatively focused on the big question for modern Christianity. Namely, how can we reshape and release the Church to be as influential on Monday as it is on Sunday? Unless we close this gap the Church will drift away as an irrelevant artifact of the past. This book can prevent such a drift!"
    – **Dr. Robert J. Rhoden**, Celebration Church and Outreach Ministry, Richmond, VA

"An extremely practical book on a complex subject! Dr. Papazov has not written a book based on theory or history, but a manual on hands-on experiences of both her ministry and of others' of like persuasion of market-place ministry. For many readers, to gain the maximum benefit from reading the book, will demand the willingness to lay aside past prejudices and even more difficult, the resistance to surrender to change. The results of this paradigm shift in envisioning and evaluating ministry speak for themselves! I highly recommend this book to those in ministry who are willing to have their goals and methodology challenged."

– **Dr. Gary Royer**, Professor, Intercultural Studies, Southwestern Assemblies of God University, Waxahachie, Texas

"Church for Monday opens our imagination to how apprentices of Jesus are equipped within local church community to live more integrally into God's mission during the week. Insightful, innovative, entrepreneurial and practical, Church For Monday is a welcome and timely contribution to the faith, work and economic movement. I recommend it."

– **Tom Nelson**, President Made to Flourish, Overland Park, KS

It's well known that Christians traditionally gather for worship on Sunday. What's less clear is how Sunday worship connects to the other six days of the week. In *Church for Monday*, Svetlana clearly and powerfully unpacks how the gathered church on Sunday becomes the scattered church the rest of the week. This isn't just another book about marketplace ministry (though that is critical), it's about how the people of God can be salt and light in the community, empowered by the Holy Spirit to reconcile their neighbors, co-workers and families to Jesus. Every pastor should read this and put it into practice."

– **John Davidson, Ph.D.**, Director - Alliance for AG Higher Education and Director - Church Multiplication Network Leadership Development, AG National Office, Springfield, MO

"With the wisdom of a pastor, the expertise of an entrepreneur, the passion of an educator, and the theological accuracy of a Bible scholar, Dr. Svetlana Papazov, in *Church for Monday*, diagnoses the current state of the Church and offers a biblical remedy for her cure...equip every Christian how to minister in their place of employment and find true enjoyment while doing it! Church for Monday fills the 40 hour a week void left unaddressed by the majority of the Church leaders!"

– **Dr. Jamie Morgan**, Lead Pastor, Life Church, Williamstown, NJ

"Dr. Papazov has a delightful writing style that is immediately engaging. Her stories are engaging and her message relevant to every believer. She challenges common perceptions in the American Church and has a unique perspective from her life behind the Iron Curtain. Her insightful work provides questions for reflection to help readers apply the truths to their own lives. While her message is intense and comprehensive, it is not burdensome. She teaches kingdom entrepreneurship in a way that makes it attainable for people of all ages and backgrounds. The practical steps she provides will allow anyone in any size church to make immediate application and begin meeting needs in their communities in order to transform lives."

– **Kimberly J. Bernecker**, E.D., Vice President for Institutional Effectiveness, Southwestern Assembly of God University, Waxahachie, TX

"Many of us who love the church know that all is not well. While some congregations are growing explosively, many others are in decline, aging and seemingly irrelevant to the communities that surround them. While the worldwide church is growing at unprecedented rates, church membership is declining at alarming rates in the USA. Likely there will be many new models developed to address this decline, but one worth serious consideration is the Church for Monday model put forward in this excellent book. Dr. Svetlana Papazov's writing is easy to read, applicable, and challenging. It will whet your appetite for how church can be reimagined to bring the marketplace and ministry together in very innovative ways that can help both the church and the community flourish."

– **Ivan L. Filby, PhD**, President - Greenville University, Greenville IL

"In a *Church for Monday*, my colleague, sister and consummate entrepreneur Svetlana Papazov, helps Jesus' bride, the church, to think, to imagine, and to act missionally, entrepreneurially, socially, economically, culturally, spiritually, and discerningly in the best interests of her communities and her neighbors, including those neighbors in the marketplace. Svetlana reminds us that thinking, imagining, and acting Christianly and God-honorably, begins at home base: the church, God's all-of-life training facility. It is here, we must relentlessly inculcate Christian virtue; it is here, we must cast an expansive Christian vision for the sake of the world; and it is here, we must faithfully equip all-of-life disciple-apprentices. Thankfully, Dr. Papazov shows us the way in this timely book."

–. **Luke Bobo**, Director of Partner Engagement, Made to Flourish, Overland Park, KS

"*Church for Monday* is a clarion call for the Church to engage each person, whether young or old, to release their God-given imagination to make an impact outside the walls of the church for the benefit of their community. In this book you will find practical tools that will awaken the creative imagination of the church to learn how their people and property can be used to love their neighbors and help them flourish. *Church for Monday* is not about adding one more thing to do on your calendar; it is learning how to be intentional in your spheres of influence to live as the everyday people of God ready to share the love and hope of Christ in useful and meaningful ways."

– **Rev. Dr. Laura Shannon McDaniel**, Network Catalyst, Uptick

"In today's culture there is an ever-widening gap between church on Sunday and work on Monday. Dr. Svetlana Papazov closes that gap by equipping believers to be more aware of what God is doing around and through them every day—not just on Sunday. Using stories and personal experience, Dr. Papazov draws in her readers while giving them concrete ways to reimagine church. A definite must read for anyone searching for a relevant church experience."

– **Edie Melson**, Director of the Blue Ridge Mountains Christian Writers Conference and Author of the Soul Care series

"The world today is tired of segmented religion—church on Sunday and real life the rest of the week. Dr. Svetlana Papazov bridges that gap with practical application, heart-warming stories and winsome transparency. Svetlana's insight will change the way— for the better—of how we approach church. This is a needed book for today and will reach those who are active in a traditional church setting and those who are searching for new ways to reach the marketplace."

– **Rod Loy**, Senior Pastor, First Assembly of God, North Little Rock, AR and Author of *Three Questions, Immediate Obedience, After the Honeymoon, Help, I'm in Charge!*

"What an incredible vision Dr. Svetlana Papazov created through her church. Real Life Church inspires others to understand their earthly, God-given purpose. This new concept incorporates a person's faith into the rest of their life. If you are involved in a church that wants to expand its doors and equip its congregation to enlarge their boundaries into their community and marketplace, this book is for you."

– **Susan Neal RN, MBA, MHS**, Award-winning author of *7 Steps to Get Off Sugar and Carbohydrates*

"Dr. Papazov's passionate entrepreneurial spirit shines through in this work as she seeks to lay out a road map for bridging the sacred/secular divide. She does a great job of presenting a theologically sound and practical plan for the church and thoughtful Christians to pursue the integration of faith and work. Whether you're a church leader or just the average Christian struggling to close the Sunday to Monday gap, this book will help you to re-connect the Christian faith with the 9-to-5 work day."

– **Brandon Nickisch, M.A.** Practical Theology and U.S. Government Training Systems Test Engineer

"*Church for Monday* is a book that will awaken your imagination and ignite a passion in your heart to close the gap between faith and work. This book will help you see the people you interact with each day as more than just casual acquaintances, but as those whom God has placed in your life to experience His love."

– **Jeff Greer**, Senior Pastor, Grace Chapel, Mason, OH

"Dr. Svetlana Papazov understands the intersection and deep interconnectedness of Faith and Work. Her *Church for Monday* will equip men and women to walk out their faith and bind their Bibles in leather...shoe leather."

– **Dr. Scott Camp**, Author, Educator, Evangelist and Host of "The Conversation" with Scott Camp, Arlington, TX

"The Church in America needs to awaken to the realization that there is a culture that needs the transforming power of the Gospel in positive, convincing, and determined ways. Our culture is at odds with our convictions and we need to step forward. *Church for Monday* is not just another book to encourage Christians to live out their faith outside of the four walls of the church. Svetlana Papazov has given us a roadmap to joyfully accomplish this important task. All of us stand to benefit deeply from the wisdom in this important book.

– **Ismael Hernancez**, Executive Director, Freedom & Virtue Institute

"The contemporary North American church finds itself amidst great changes, particularly in the area of economics. Dr. Svetlana Papazov outlines these changes and gives insight for churches to successfully navigate through them to fulfill the mission of God. She not only provides a needed perspective for the church's role in the marketplace, she also offers practical examples from churches across the country that are leading the way forward. This book needs to be read and digested by church leaders to help them envision new possibilities for the church in the 21st century."

– **Dr. W. Jay Moon**, Director, Office of Faith, Work, and Economics, Asbury Theological Seminary and Professor, Intercultural Studies

Church for Monday

Equipping Believers for Mission at Work

By
Svetlana Papazov

Living Parables Publishers
Oviedo, Florida

Copyright © 2019 by Svetlana Papazov

Cover Design by Amber Weigand-Buckley,
Barefaced Creative Global Brand.
Author Photos by Bryan Papazov, www.instagRam.com/bryanpapazov

Published by Living Parables
1567 Thornhill Circle
Oviedo FL 32765

Living Parables is a division of
EABooks Publishing and Living Parables of
Central Florida, Inc. a 501c3

Quantity sales. Special discounts are available on quantity purchases by corporations, associations, and others. For details, contact the publisher at the address above. Orders by U.S. trade bookstores and wholesalers. Please contact Anchor Distributors.

Publisher's Cataloging-in-Publication data
Name: Papazov, Svetlana
Title: Church for Monday: Equipping Believers for Mission at Work| Sveltana Papazov.
Identifiers: LCCN 2019911060| ISBN 978-1-945976-50-6
Subjects: 1. The main category of the book —Religion: Christian Church/ Growth. 2. Other category— Christian Living / Calling & Vocation. 3. Another subject category — Christian Ministry / Missions.

All Scripture quotations, unless otherwise marked, are taken from the Holy Bible, NEW INTERNATIONAL VERSION (NIV): Scripture taken from THE HOLY BIBLE, NEW INTERNATIONAL VERSION ®. Copyright© 1973, 1978, 1984, 2011 by Biblica, Inc.™. Used by permission of Zondervan

(While any stories in this book are true, some names and identifying information may have been changed to protect the privacy of individuals.)
First Edition
Printed in the United States of America

Dedication

I dedicate this book to my amazing husband, Michael,

My greatest supporter in life,

A godly example of love and kindness,

My faithful partner in all good things accomplished.

Contents

Foreword

It is a fact that you probably aren't aware of yet, but you will be soon. In the next decade or so more than half of all churches in the United States are likely going to close their doors forever.

The reasons for these closures aren't going to arise as a result of the church's radical political affiliations, well documented theological disagreements, disinterest in institutional religion, or even a sudden lack of belief in God. No, the church has faced similar contextual issues all throughout her rich history.

The coming challenge is something that the church has never faced before. It is a challenge that will impact every aspect of humanity and change the very foundations as to how we view ourselves. Consequently, it will also impact how we view ourselves in relationship to God.

So, what is this unnamed obstacle? What is this potential destruction of the institutional church? It's robots... specifically the coming automation crisis.

Now before you declare me a loon, allow me to explain. The very best report on automation of the world – by the McKinsey Global Institute – predicts that in a decade there will be a global automation crisis that will disrupt economies and culture in unprecedented ways. In the US alone they predict that there will be 11-22% job loss with that percentage only increasing over time. At 22% unemployment, the United States will be facing its greatest unemployment rate since The Great Depression. And remember, this won't just impact the United States; it will be a global phenomenon.

How will this impact the church in the United States? Well, 57% of churches in the US are less than 100 members and many struggle to support a full-time pastor. Even at 11% unemployment – many of these churches will cease being able to employ a pastor or maintain the upkeep of their facilities. Churches that are property heavy (like many mega-churches) will begin to feel the burden of this increasing unemployment rate and will likely have to make radical changes to how they operate. Many small churches will simply not be able to afford to keep operating. Beyond this, when a large percentage of the world's people will need the care and nurture of the church the most, churches that don't prepare for this coming crisis will find themselves permanently sidelined.

As a lead global clergy expert regarding Artificial Intelligence, I have had the privilege of advising politicians and meeting with some of the top AI experts in the world. Behind the scenes, they are all talking about the coming AI crisis like it is a meteor headed towards earth and Bruce Willis is nowhere to be found. What they are unsure about is whether they should tell the general public about what is coming or not. They don't want to insight panic, but they also know that the general populace is wildly unprepared for what is coming.

What makes this impending international calamity even worse is that the social institution that is best oriented to aid in assisting people in crisis at a local level will be critically debilitated if it doesn't start preparing right now. It is already the case that many churches across the country have failed to leverage their institutional legacies as a way to foster creativity to enable future flourishing. They have failed to become self-sustainable. Now they are potentially facing large-scale institutional extinction.

This is a problem because without the help of the local church, people will unnecessarily suffer. During prior widespread disasters such as the Great Depression, the institution of the church has served as a steadfast place of encouragement for those in need. When people found themselves in desperation and despair, the institution of the church served as a refuge of hope and a reimagined source of ultimate meaning. When the masses questioned their identity in the face of disruptive change the church creatively found ways to point people towards the transformative God of new Creation. When practical needs had to be met to alleviate suffering – the church actively sought to provide much needed assistance.

To be perfectly clear, the issue of unemployment related to the coming automation crisis is not that there won't be new jobs available. The problem will be that people won't be able to retrain for them quickly enough to prevent mass chaos. In a world already consumed with conflict-methodology it doesn't take much imagination to envision how such a disruption could send the whole world into chaos.

But it doesn't have to go that way.

In her book, *Church for Monday*, Dr. Svetlana Papazov gives a hopeful glimpse and practical tools of how the church universal, and your church specifically, can be a counter to this crisis and many others along the way. You can help people to learn to out-create automation and lean into an identity that they are made in the image of a Creator God. Svetlana's work articulates a fact that most churches will need to adopt in the next decade if they want to maintain cultural relevancy and continue on as religious institutions bearing fruit—the church has to close the Sunday-to-Monday gap and integrate itself in the marketplace.

If you embrace her invitation to integrated faith, you'll find that the value of *Church for Monday* is not that it will serve as an echo chamber to reinforce your current theological assertions. I rarely agree with anyone I meet on all theological issues. I'm good with that fact because all theology has a context and what I have discovered over the years is that my context is often very different than those around me. But if you grasp this book's underlying concepts, it has the potential to allow you and your church to more fully experience what it means to be made in the Image of the Triune God - Creator, Redeemer, and Spirit, and maybe more importantly still, to begin a process for your church that may help alleviate and even prevent future suffering in the world.

You can help people to more fully participate in the redemptive purposes of Christ.

You can help people and your church to flourish.

You can make your church self-sustainable.

But you have to start somewhere. *Church for Monday* can serve as a great place to start...

Rev. Dr. Christopher J. Benek, Pastor & CEO – CoCreators
Pastor – First Miami Presbyterian Church

Definitions of Terms

For many, the terms I use will be familiar, but because definitions are sometimes different, I offer this list so we can begin from the same place.

Church for Monday is a term used for churches that close the Sunday-to-Monday gap by uniting worship on Sunday to work on Monday. These churches prepare believers to partner with God in His mission, not only abroad, but also in their own backyard. Churches that equip for Monday seek sustainable ways to grow spiritually, socially, and economically. They translate the gospel for the postmodern world, develop whole-life-disciples, and strategically embed themselves in the marketplace by developing the gifts and talents of their constituencies.

Such churches have grown in the awareness that as the gap between practicing Christians and the unchurched has dangerously widened, the 8-to-5 window (the work day), has become a mission field as important as the 10/40 window (a geographical area with high concentrations of unreached people for Christ) because the workplace is where the majority of unchurched people spend the majority of their waking hours.

Biblical Transformation or ***Transformation,*** as it will be referred to in this book, is a change from a condition of human existence lived contrary to God's creation purpose to a condition in which individuals and cultures experience fullness of life in harmony with God (John 10:10). This concept refers to the holistic change that happens in those who respond to the salvation grace of Jesus Christ and submit to his lordship. Although *biblical transformation* begins as a personal experience, its impact on humans takes it from a private lifestyle to social and economic reality.

Transformational Development is a Spirit-empowered process through which persons and cultures experience spiritual, social, and economic change.

Culture in this book is taken in its wide ethnocentric sense and adopts Edward B. Tylor's definition for culture or civilization: "That complex whole which includes knowledge, belief, art, law, morals, custom, and any other capabilities and habits acquired by man as a member of society" [1]

Postmodernism is a worldview that denies any absolute truth while also embracing philosophical, ideological, and moral relativism, including the embracing of pluralism (many ways to God) and many alternate lifestyle options.

Missio Dei is a Latin Christian theological term that means the mission of God in human history.

Asset-Based Community Development (ABCD) is a methodology that seeks to uncover and utilize the strengths within communities as a means for development. It helps communities become stronger and more self-reliant by discovering, mapping, and mobilizing all their local assets to solve problems.

Acknowledgments

Thank you to:
All the pastors who contributed their local church stories so I can
paint a picture of what's possible for the global church—Scott
Woller, Jeff Greer, Jamé Bolds, John Cruz, Mark DeYmaz, Fernando
Tamara, Keith Case, Dan Davidson, and Tyler Chernesky;

All the thought leaders and practitioners who envisioned with me in
the Foreword, Afterword, and Chapter 10 how the church can regain
relevance in the marketplace—Christopher Benek, Mark DeYmaz,
Tom Nelson, Steve Pike, Senator Amanda Chase, Chuck Proudfit,
Leah Archibald, Karley Hatter, David Kinnaman and the Barna Group,
Cassandra Ferguson, Linda Evans Shepherd, Mark Roberts, and Tom
Thatcher;

Our Real Life Church family that I have the privilege of serving and
joyfully partner with to discover new ways for marketplace
engagement;

My husband Michael whose dedicated hard work behind the scenes
was instrumental to see this project completed on time;

Kelly Ward, my friend, parishioner, digital marketer, and tireless
proofreader;

Lacey Self, our Real Life's Creative Director and my plate catcher—
making sure I wouldn't drop the many spinning plates I juggled while
writing;

Cheri Cowell, my gracious publisher, who recognized the message in
the messenger and gave me a chance to tell my story to impact the
story of others, and Peter Lundell, my developmental editor who
made this manuscript better than I imagined;

The many wise and caring friends whose endorsements, prayers,
and insights have shaped what you find in this book;

Grateful to my Lord....

PART ONE

FAITHFUL
REORIENTATION

Getting a Vision

Awakened to Dream

Eight-year-old Jeremiah sported fashionable, orange-colored hair, and had come with his mother to Real Life Church. I enjoyed the controlled chaos and especially the bobbing heads of kids exchanging pictures, crayons, and stories in our KidPreneurs camp— an incubator for children five to twelve in which they explored God's purpose for their lives through entrepreneurship. Everyone was engaged except for Jeremiah. He wasn't searching for colorful pictures, cutting, or gluing like the other kids. He only stared at the poster paper in front of him—not a single picture glued, not a single word spelling out his dream. Much younger kids were already cutting shapes and drawing their squiggly lines, laughing and gluing pictures of beaches, mansions, and lemonade stands. But Jeremiah seemed paralyzed by the assigned task—to simply dream.

I knelt beside him and asked, "What is your hope for the future, my friend? What are your dreams?" He looked at me and said bluntly, "I'm not dreaming about anything."

Jeremiah, like many of the other kids there that day, came from some rough circumstances and lived in an economic desert, disconnected from hope in a society and a God who cared. This is why we were here. This was our purpose.

I tried again. "What I'm saying is, what are the things that you really want to share with your friends?" He said, "I don't want to do any of that." I wasn't sure if I could awaken the dreamer in him, but I ventured one more time. "Listen, when you play, do you like sports?" He looked at me and said, "Uh, I kind of like sports and kind of don't because when it rains and the fields get muddy, I can't play football."

A thought came to mind and I went with it. "Oh, the fields! The fields are muddy and stopping you from playing, right?" He nodded. "How would you like to solve that problem—to play even when it has rained? Don't you think many people will be grateful that you thought of a better way?" For the first time, he looked at me with interest. "Uh-huh." A deep sense of relief came over me. "How about if you and I dream of something to put down so that when it rains you and your friends can play? Kind of like that green outdoor carpet." I pointed to the greenish colored carpet in the other room.

Jeremiah's face lit up. He didn't need my help anymore. He took the magazines and began to look for green stuff, carpets, and things that he could cut, paste, and draw. Jeremiah's vision was unleashed. His blank poster now burst with colorful pieces of his imagination. Hope for the future was being birthed, and an entrepreneurial mindset was emerging. Because, to think entrepreneurially, all a person needs to do is to come up with a viable solution to a problem.

Dr. Douglas Melton, Director for the Entrepreneurial Engineering Program at The Kern Family Foundation, says that a person with an entrepreneurial mindset is an agent of change and designs the world of tomorrow.[1] It is my contention that God strategically positions believers for influence in business, education, government, media, arts and entertainment, family, and religion. Then God sends us on His mission as agents of change in the world around us. God, the Ultimate Entrepreneur who has fashioned everything out of nothing, has formed everyone uniquely in order to co-create with Him redeemed futures for humanity (Jeremiah 29:11). If we pay attention to the beckoning of the Holy Spirit, we can act in an entrepreneurial manner and partner with God in His work in the world. I have come to understand that the church cannot transform its communities if it stays disengaged from society, playing "church" with its own Lego blocks. If you are reading this book, I'm sure you agree and are one of the change agents I'm describing. You, too, believe that the body of Christ is called to be a living, prophetic, tangible model of the Great Commission. That statement is one you've, no doubt, read before. However, the second part of that statement is one you may not have heard and it is what this book is about—the church is called to be a living, prophetic, tangible model of the Great Commission *by integrating faith, creativity, and mission in the marketplace.*

This book will demonstrate a church model of how we can share God's grace and talents, which are available in each of us, with our communities. As you will see, when we disciple people for the whole of life we usher godly transformation into all spheres of society. Thankfully, the churches that are missionally engaging their communities are on the rise. If your church hasn't started on that journey yet, don't fret. Through the stories, in this book you will be encouraged and learn how to re-tool what you are already doing to be more impactful as missional instruments in the marketplace. The New Testament church saw itself as a disruptor. It accepted the call of Jesus to enter all sectors of society across the world, not just on Sunday but also on Monday, in order to share the gospel with love and courageous innovation. Following the New Testament model, the contemporary church should be emboldened to live faithfully for Christ in the public arena, not because everyone understands the church, but because the church understands the need of everyone: a need of a Savior from wrecked existence and a need of a Healer from human suffering.

After more than a decade serving as a full-time pastor and equipping different churches for mission in the marketplace, I have observed that a church that trains for mission-at-work and closes the perilous Sunday-to-Monday gap is not a "how" church but a "why" church. That type of church has a mindset that is not about methodology, but about the praxis of Christology, about modeling itself after "the Word becoming flesh and blood and moving into the neighborhood" (John 1:14 MSG), in order to practice a corporate, contextualized expression of the Great Commission. As we will learn, this kind of mindset helps churches love their cities well through three priorities: *first, translating the gospel for those who we'll call the unchurched—those who have little or no church experience; second, deploying disciples who attend to the whole of life in all sectors of society; and third, strategically placing disciples in the marketplace to impact the economic health of their communities.*

You will be encouraged that churches wanting to lead entrepreneurially in the mission of God and become an integral part of the society prepare themselves on Sunday to bridge their faith into the workweek on Monday. What if your church were to fully embrace this vision and train the Jeremiahs of all ages, young and old, to dream, create and contribute? What if the neighborly love your church professes found an economic aspect and pushed into the mission field of the marketplace on the outside of your church walls?

There is already a burgeoning number of churches embedded in the economy but what will happen if more local churches awaken to the necessity of establishing its faithful presence in the marketplace? We know people spend the majority of their time outside of church each week. What if the church was present during those hours? Can the church meet the curiosity of our next generation with environments that dare them to dream and create? What if we unleashed our members to equip our children—the future of our society, especially in economically vulnerable communities—to dream, create, and contribute to this future? According to the Barna Research Group, the time before the age of thirteen is when people are most prone to accept and act upon the salvation message. [2] The future of the American Church and our nation hinges on reaching our children with a holistic gospel. For that matter, the future of any nation depends on how well it reaches their next generation for Jesus Christ.

As I watched Jeremiah awaken the dreams within him as he sought to solve a problem he understood in his own community, I imagined him one day walking the hallways of his high school, confident in his human dignity and entrepreneurial mindset. Can you see the hallways of your city's high school bursting at the seams with graduates ready to dream, create, and contribute to society just like Jeremiah? Can you see the potential for the spiritual, economic, and social lift both in vulnerable and economically developed communities if your church enters them on a holistic mission? Jesus says that the Father is always working (John 5:17). His creative and redeeming work is needed both in poverty-stricken and in wealthy countries. What would it take to unleash the potential of creative, working Jeremiahs, young and old, across our nation and beyond in a relationship with a creative Christ?

Living the Dream

Like young Jeremiah, I too grew up in the bondage of a spiritual, entrepreneurial, and economic desert—although I lived behind the Iron Curtain where entrepreneurs were punished by law. My mom was one of them. But in his grace, God unleashed my imagination through one of my professors who stirred within me a hunger for more. When I heard of the freedom those in the United States had, I knew I had to get there. Through hard work, my quest for free expression of the human spirit eventually brought me to the U.S. Once here, I immediately started my own business of a design-build firm utilizing my graduate degree in landscape architecture. The first business was such a success, my husband and I opened three more—a garden center, florist shop, and a gift store. Yet, I still carried my youthful dream to finish a biblical degree, a dream unattainable in Communist countries. So, once we were financially stable, I took full advantage of this American opportunity and furthered my education at Christian institutions by finishing a second Master's in Theology, and a Doctorate of Ministry in Leadership.

As I worked, I realized not everyone saw the gift of freedom to create as the God-calling that I did. I was puzzled by the way in which followers of Christ casually approached this opportunity to co-create with God. I knew I had a unique perspective coming from a place where what American Christians took for granted was outlawed. So, as the Lord led my husband and me into church leadership, and I transitioned from a businesswoman into an ordained minister, we determined our focus would be on connecting our members to God's plan to integrate work and faith—doing real life with real people, connecting them to the real God in order to see a spiritual, social, and economic transformation not just on Sunday but on Monday and throughout the week.

During my first pastorate at a large church in the Dallas, TX metroplex, I was privileged to work with ethnically diverse, vision-driven believers who, although living in scarcity, didn't allow that to limit or define God's plan for them. These people became our

Jeremiahs. As we worked side-by-side, I soon saw the needs in this community were not just spiritual. Many in the community were living in survival mode. They needed good jobs, but some had criminal records, and many lacked the education or skills needed to secure stable, better-paying employment. I knew I couldn't stay on the sidelines when it came to their work situation and only speak about the matters of their spirit —for me it all went together. My decision to help came in the form of education and encouragement. I began by turning Wednesday night services into training sessions, where I taught the biblical concepts of leadership, entrepreneurship, and economics, sharing with our congregation the same principles I taught as a professor in the business department of a Christian university in town.

During that time, our congregation grew. People's entrepreneurial skills increased as they prayed, explored God-sized visions for their lives, and learned valuable steps in how to open a business. There were many Jeremiahs that experienced upward mobility—some found employment and better jobs, while others started their own businesses. Still today, I treasure a note I received from a young Hispanic couple that came faithfully to these mid-week services. When they started their own business they sent a message to express gratitude for the way the church loved them because we were concerned for their family's economic life and gave them practical help to improve their living conditions and their place in society. Now, this couple is a tangible representation of the love of God in the marketplace as business owners who train students in job skills for the dental industry.

During my second pastorate at a well-established, mid-sized church in Maryland sixty miles from Washington, D.C., I saw similar economic needs in the surrounding community. The Holy Spirit impressed me to reach out to local schools in these distressed areas so my team and I could work with families. We knew that while helping parents improve the quality of their lives, we could also train the children in skills needed for their school work. We found a school full of Jeremiahs, young and old, who welcomed our church to lead them toward an economic lift. Our church volunteers were allowed to work with the parents and students on the school premises after school hours. My vision was to bridge the gap of the secular and sacred divide through a Faith and Public School Partnership Prototype, which our team developed. We used this program to train students and parents in employability skills, financial savviness, and goal setting.

The Partnership Prototype's structure centered upon two foundational modules: a development track and a transformational track. The development track addressed the social and economic lift, whereas the transformational track addressed the spiritual change in the participants. In the development track for adults, we taught goal setting, financial intelligence, and job readiness courses. The children's curriculum included fun activities and biblical instruction that followed the adults' curriculum thematically to facilitate common family discussions on financial stewardship and life's goals. The development track was a way to build the bridge to the community and lift it economically, while the transformational track made the pivotal difference in people's spiritual state.

The transformational track consisted of three main elements: intercessory prayer, Christian value-based curricula, and relational connectors. Perhaps the most important aspect of our program was prayer. Before our weekly training our volunteers walked the school praying. In addition, other church intercessors prayed for the school throughout the week. Christian values undergirded all curricula and one-on-one relationships were formed with the participants. Intentionally, several of the volunteers attended the instructions not as facilitators but as connectors—becoming friends with the parents. Because we shaped relationships, many came to our Sunday services, and several accepted Christ.

After we'd been at the school for six months, training and supporting both the parents and the students, the assistant principal told us that they could sense the entire atmosphere of the school changing. In addition, the parents who were participating in our partnership prototype began to ask us how they could help their neighbors as we had helped them.

During my years as a small business owner, I had become keenly aware that most of my clients never asked themselves which local church they will go to on Sunday morning. Talking about church and God were conversations that many of them carefully avoided. Since then the desire to find effective ways for the church to reconnect or possibly connect for the first time unchurched people to God has been my ministry goal.

Right before I transitioned from a small business owner to a pastor, during a lengthy session of prayer, I had a vision of something that on the outside looked like businesses but on the inside looked like a church—it was a vision of the marketplace and the church was placed in the middle of it. What God showed me was a confirmation of what I had begun to understand—that whole-life discipleship integrates faith into work and economics. If we separate biblical principles such as creativity, human dignity, and stewardship from the workplace, we set our cities up for failure. Although I had never seen anything like my vision, I knew that God was calling my husband and me to meld church and work, economics and entrepreneurship, in a practical way. I faithfully applied these concepts in my pastorates in Texas and Maryland and in the founding and pastoring of an entrepreneurial church in Virginia.

In order to close the Sunday-to-Monday gap between church and the marketplace in a way that would allow us to duplicate, my husband Michael and I, with a team of supporters, started Real Life Church. [3] Our team is doing missional work among businesses and entrepreneurs.

In our desire to be embedded in the economy of our city and bridge the sacred and secular divide in a practical way, Real Life Church opened Real Life Center for Entrepreneurial and Leadership Excellence—a business incubator that prepares people for their occupations. The Entrepreneurial Center trains in leadership and entrepreneurship to give unchurched people the opportunity to experience God and faith outside of Sunday as we lift our community economically, socially, and spiritually. We care for our community and contribute to our local economy by guiding people to identify and develop their gifts and skills in order to lead well at their jobs, hire new employees, or start new businesses. In addition, we do business incubation, offer co-working space and private offices for work, business consulting, networking to identify new job opportunities, educational workshops, and adult and next-generation entrepreneurial training. Most of these functions are facilitated by church volunteers skilled to equip in these various ways.

We have found that developing people's entrepreneurial skills sets them up for success and unleashes their potential. Having a problem-solving mentality, with a growth-oriented mindset, one can do well anywhere: at home, at school, at work, in government, and in business. For that reason, we have created faith and entrepreneurship programs for kids, teens, and adults. The programs of Real Life KidPreneurs and Real Life TeenPreneurs as summer camps, Beyond VBS, and school classroom curricula have been effective in fostering next-generation creativity. The Real Life AdultPreneurs program trains in business and entrepreneurial skills for adults interested in starting their own businesses and also for those affected by the opioid crisis and in at-risk situations. During our Kid, Teen, and AdultPreneurs programs, we have repeatedly discovered and unleashed our Jeremiahs to dream, create, and contribute.

Although our real estate has a small footprint, we believe we can make a big difference with it. Real Life's small building of 3,200 sq. ft. has provided co-working space and offices for more than a dozen businesses. One such business owner is Pam, a financial professional who came to us when she couldn't afford her own building. The local coffee shops no longer fit her clients' needs. She was in that in-between stage where many entrepreneurs do not make it. The Real Life incubator supports entrepreneurs by offering private offices in vulnerable times of too-fast-growth and not-enough-capacity. In our facilities and in our programs, Pam has found a place to belong, grow, and steward hundreds of thousands of dollars for her clients. She has hired four employees, and her impact on the economy has increased because Real Life supports small business owners with entrepreneurial environments and low cost rent.

In addition to offering private offices, we facilitate business training based on biblical principles. Hundreds of adult entrepreneurs have been trained at Real Life through workshops, masterminds, business coaching, networking, and caring relationships. In this way, we empower for greater contribution to our local economy. Moreover, we have unleashed the imaginations of hundreds of children through the Real Life KidPreneurs and TeenPreneurs programs.

Spurred into creativity, Zoe and her older sister, Chloe, launched a small business called Knicks and Knacks after finishing the Real Life KidPreneurs summer camp. Together, they have developed a line of goods with teens and preteens in mind. These are two young entrepreneurs who are not waiting to become adults in order to dream, create, and contribute to our local economy. In all of our training, we focus on developing an entrepreneurial mindset with a biblical worldview. We teach that business dreams can have a social and economic impact on the real world and the real economy. We help adults and kids reverse-engineer their dreams into strategic business plans that they can launch now.

The majority of the people in our church startup have joined because of faith and entrepreneurship integration. Kelly, a digital marketing expert, re-connected to God and faith and is now a committed member of our church because she was looking for a space to expand her business and rented an office at Real Life. Liza came to our Christmas Small Business Open House Expo as a vendor. The next Sunday she came to church and recommitted her life to Christ. Now her kids, too, have become a part of the church. Terry is a freelance photographer who one Sunday came on our property to take pictures of his client. As my husband and I approached him, he thought he would get in trouble because of trespassing. To his surprise, we welcomed him to utilize not just the outside of our property, but the business incubator as well, by doing photoshoots in one of our vacant offices. That deeply impacted him, and Terry and his wife came back to Real Life, this time to church, and there they found a genuine church family that has welcomed them home. Terry's photography business has also expanded since joining our Real Life church community. These are only a few of the many lives that have been touched through Real Life's integration of faith and entrepreneurship.

Patient Work with Lasting Impact

As grateful as we are for each individual transformation, and as rewarding as the work of faith integration is, the Real Life Church has experienced steady—but what would seem to most— slow growth. Although we minister through entrepreneurial events, workshops, networking, coaching, and consulting, this work is not a convert-producing machine. As a church planter, I was tempted to compare the attendance numbers of our organic church start to the attendance numbers of some who had made national headlines as fast-growing church plants that began with lots of money and big groups of transfer Christians. And although in the first three years we experienced more than fifty-five salvations, I considered our attendance numbers to be a failure. That was until I reminded myself to be patient and see our work for what it is—a missionary work. We are not reaching practicing Christians or church hoppers, we are reaching the lapsed and non-churched. I call them nones— people who are away from God and church. Barna identifies the lapsed as people who have not been in church for more than a month (our own experience is that they have not been in church for several years, with the exception of holidays) and of whom only four-percent consider their faith very important. The nones do not identify with any faith, or if they do, it is not Christian. [4]

What we have found out is that people, who have not been in church for years, or never, are slow to warm up to the gospel and need time to make a lasting decision for Christ. To encourage my heart, for a season I had to stop counting Sunday numbers and re-focus my attention on counting the numbers we were reaching in the Sunday-to-Monday connect bridge. This simple act reframed my thinking about our church's scorecard.

If someone is looking for a fast church-growth model, the entrepreneurial church is not it. There is nothing fast when we are building Church for Monday. This church must be thoughtful and patient in order to affect lasting transformation, otherwise, people begin to feel bulldozed into grace and will reject our witness. Personally, I see this approach as closer to God's intent than impressive numbers generated by well-financed starts populated by believers transferring from established churches.

As word got out about what we were doing, churches, organizations, universities, church planting networks, and denominational districts started reaching out for training and coaching in translating the gospel for the unchurched, in equipping believers for whole-life discipleship, and in strategic envisioning for embedding churches in the marketplace for economic impact. Because of the extensive work I've done in the faith and work arena, the Made to Flourish [5] organization—a nationwide network that empowers pastors and their churches to integrate faith, work and economic wisdom for the flourishing of their communities—felt that my experience would be of value to their East Coast network in Richmond, Virginia, and asked me to be their representative as City Network Leader there. In addition, I serve as faculty at the Acton University [6]—a unique annual forum of thousands of global leaders from over ninety countries that gather to explore the intersection between faith and the marketplace. Giving leadership to the Richmond Made to Flourish network, teaching at Acton University, training and coaching for organizations such as Church Multiplication Network [7] and Mosaix [8] and other forerunners in the faith integration movement has been rewarding work, presenting me with the opportunity not only to equip leaders but also to learn from the mavericks novel ways to bridge the marketplace gap.

I believe that if the church embeds itself in the community as the incarnate love of Christ, it will see the Jeremiahs waiting to be reached. In the coming chapters I want you to keep these questions centered in your heart and mind:

Where are your Jeremiahs? Are you entering their economic gates? How are you and your church creatively engaging them?

It is my prayer that when you finish this book you will know who your Jeremiahs are and have a plan to engage them. May your church decide it will become a *Church for Monday*.

What Is a Church for Monday?

The Beginning

What does the future of the church look like? This is the question that will be discussed for at least the next decade. With it, we must also ask, how can we be a faithful church that prepares God's people for the majority of their lives that is led on Monday not Sunday? Said another way, in what ways can the church navigate the complexities of our current culture *and* regain a seat in the public arena? Finally, can we invite the Holy Spirit to stir our imagination to envision a path forward?

You won't read in this chapter or this book about the magic bullet for church growth, or the remedy for all that is wrong with church and society. Instead, I'll offer you an evaluation of where we are in regards to our calling in the world, and how to missionally align our vision for the future of the church. Church for Monday is not a fad, or the latest new thing, rather, it is a concept that comes from a deep theological conviction of how God created us, His plan of redemption, and the importance of work and calling in that plan.

We all know that things are changing, but the question is how fast and how furious. It is a fact, not fear-mongering, to say that when a crisis hits, people rarely look to the church for guidance. We live in turbulent times where crime, divisiveness, and chaos seem to be the norm, and peaceful, united, and respectful discourse is a wistful memory of the past. In addition, the church in the West is suffering from a damaged public image and it finds itself ousted as the moral herald. It sits on the margins of society. Now is the time to practice public faith so as to regain relevance. But how will we do it?

Church for Monday

Churches for Monday enter the marketplace to innovate and practice public faith as both a gathered and scattered community. They prepare believers to partner with God in His mission, not only abroad, but also in their own backyard, even if they live in developed economies.

A church that equips for Monday fosters the creative streak placed in every image bearer and seeks sustainable ways to flourish the communities spiritually, socially, and economically. It translates the gospel for the postmodern world, develops whole-life disciples, and strategically embeds itself in the marketplace to grow the economy (Jer. 29:7).

A Redeeming Mandate

To recalibrate for public faith and navigate the cultural and religious complexities of the twenty-first-century marketplace is challenging but also empowering. There is a growing number of believers and church leaders who have innately known that faith separated from the rest of life does not serve any part of life. God has created us with spirit, soul, and body. He has placed us in a world that is primarily physical, not primarily spiritual. So to dichotomize the effects of redemption into spiritual versus material is to reduce the effects of salvation.

Jesus came to free his creation from the darkness that Satan brings wherever he occupies. Therefore, we are to reenter all sectors of society for Christ's sake, because all nations are Jesus' inheritance, and the ends of the earth are His possession (Psalm 2:8). This means that all the spheres of life that his inheritance (all of us) inhabits rightfully belong to Jesus. He infills us with the Holy Spirit's power and sends us to go everywhere human feet go so we can redeem His lands by making whole-life disciples.

There is so much dispute, discouragement, and deprivation in the marketplace, but we must remember that wherever we work, lead, or minister, we can approach even a secular reality in a sacred way. The enemy of our souls did not create anything but instead damaged everything. God desires to redeem all that Satan corrupts, and the church of God—this Church for Monday— is on that mission to bring the light of God into the darkest crevices of the marketplace. Because of the resurrection, all authority has been given to Jesus in all spheres of life and in all the industries of man. Nothing is beyond Jesus' authority, and for that reason, nothing is beyond the church's engagement and care (Matthew 28:18–19). Because all areas of the public arena belong to Jesus, we are commissioned to bring God's reconciling message not just to people's private lives but to the public sectors as well. The Great Commission is The Great Commandant to love the world as Jesus did. Are we willing to do it in a new way for new results?

A Model for the Future

As we know, the week has 168 hours. People spend on average only one hour at church on Sunday morning. What about the other 167 hours spent primarily at work, but also at home, and at play in a world quite intolerant of Christians, embracing other truths but opposing the truth of the Bible, enamored with narratives but rejecting the narrative of Jesus? What type of church prepares for that type of world?

The waning state of faith in young adults, the decreased attendance and weakened generosity trends, and a growing desire for person-to-person, high-touch interaction amidst high-tech connections, all point to a significant decline in both church attendance and tithes and offerings. Church, as it has been, will require re-envisioning. If Jesus tarries, what type of church will thrive, not just survive, in the following decades?

I believe the future church will be gospel-translating, experience-based, and Spirit-evident, with small congregations that grow from conversions, not church transfers. Its clergy will likely be co-vocational and willing to equip believers for their lives on Monday. It will be embedded in the marketplace, dually-using their facilities for the flourishing of the community and for their own sustainability.

The community will know the church because the church will be a part of the community—not above it, beside it, or beyond it. If anyone thinks to ask the trite question, "Will you miss the church on the corner if it closes its doors?" people will say, "Yes. I will miss that church because it trains us for meaningful work, guides us in starting new businesses, helps us make wise decisions, teaches us creative entrepreneurship, and equips us for loving parenting without insisting we first believe."

Sadly, this is rarely the answer we hear. Yet most pastors I know work long hours with little pay to make that kind of a big difference in their broken communities. So the question is not if pastors desire a marketplace impact but how to lead churches that make a lasting impact not only on weekends but on weekdays, too. How do we go there from here?

Three Main Components of the Church for Monday

An increasing number of churches are thinking creatively and preparing strategically for mission on Monday as they develop both compassion and capacity to flourish their communities. So, what does Church for Monday look like? Is intentionally integrated faith into work, economics, and entrepreneurship expressed in the same way across the local churches in our country? The answer is that Churches for Monday are as varied as the richness of their theological premises and the unique contexts they serve, but they all have three key elements: *gospel-translating, whole-life discipling, and embedding into the economy.* Before I describe what I mean by these three characteristics, I want to affirm what we all know well— we are saved through a Person, not a program. So, when we look at what we are facilitating through a Church for Monday model, I'm not advocating for programs but for creative ways we can form authentic communities where both the unchurched and the churched can enter and deepen a transforming relationship with Jesus—the Person.

Embedded in the Economy

One of the three main elements of Church for Monday is being embedded in the economy. We care for the people in our communities if we grow and strengthen their family's economic life. Gea Gort and Mats Tunehag write in their book on business as mission, "Business is the most natural way to relate to non-Christians, to live out your faith, and to disciple people." [1] It is my conviction that in order to be an impactful, twenty-first-century church, we need to connect the gospel of the kingdom with economics. Otherwise, our witness weakens, and our cities and our future will lack because we cannot separate God's formative grace from the main seedbed of culture—the economy.

If anyone doubts that the economy is important to how people live out their core values, look at the number-one issue that was on the mind of those who voted in the 2016 presidential election: 84 percent of registered voters said that the issue of the economy was very important to them in making their decision about who to vote for. [2] Should not the church be present in the dialogue about the national economy and shape its formation to exemplify the character of God? "The earth is the LORD's, and everything in it, the world, and all who live in it" (Psalm 21:1). Through work, people not only contribute tangibly to the economy of our society but through that work God forms us within. So, work and economics are two sides of a coin. That coin helps us both in developing compassion and financial capacity to love our neighbors with both a spiritual and economic lift.

Being an embedded-in-the-economy church means that such a church intentionally flourishes the economy as a gathered and scattered community. It is a given that the scattered church adds value to the economy through the members' vocations—when believers work they grow the GDP. Marketplace-embedded churches go one step further and look for ways to grow the economy as a gathered community as well. They become revenue-generating and add to the local economy by resourcing the creation of sustainable, tax-generating, charity-giving jobs and businesses; offering jobs as an employer and training for employment.

Often communities are reluctant to let a church in, either to rent or build because they see the church as not adding proactively to the economy. Most malls, shopping plazas, and similar public spaces shy away from letting churches rent at their sites because the church doesn't attract clients that add to their economic wellbeing. There is an unspoken understanding that church is allowed in shopping malls if these places are in a downturn and cannot keep any other tenants. But marketplace-embedded churches often regain trust in their communities as they add economic value, get to know the names and stories of the neighbors who work around them, and are welcomed to establish their presence in desirable public spaces.

Here are some practical ways through which pastors can begin to change the perception of their churches as a viable economic actor in the marketplace:

- Offer seed capital for new businesses launched by church members and sympathizers to faith.

- Facilitate business training based on godly virtues and biblical principles of leadership.

- Underwrite college scholarships for business degrees for the church's youth and youth from distressed communities.

- Financially and academically support under-resourced youth who will be the first in their families to seek a college education by offering capital and tutoring.

- Sponsor youth entrepreneur leadership programs to assure next-generation small business owners.

Although churches equipping for Monday develop both adults and kids, they are especially attuned to fostering next-generation creativity because kids and teens are the workforce of tomorrow and our emerging leaders. If we shape their understanding of what ministry looks like and where ministry takes place, future generations might successfully close the gap between church and the marketplace. In developing the entrepreneurial acumen in both adults and kids to see future opportunities in the markets and to launch valuable endeavors, the church unleashes human potential and teaches believers to partner with God, the Ultimate Entrepreneur. In so doing, we participate in God's providence and creative work in the world.

As I briefly discussed earlier, at Real Life we have embraced the biblical mandate for work and creativity and the importance of fostering next-generation creativity and have developed a hands-on entrepreneurial program that teaches the value of work, faith, and innovation. For kids, we offer Real Life KidPreneurs and for teens Real Life TeenPreneurs. In this program elementary, middle school, and high school students are trained in entrepreneurship in eight modules during the year. Students develop business plans and present them to friends from the community in a "Shark Tank" environment.

This is one of the ways we embed ourselves in the economy by developing young entrepreneurs that start new businesses. When Churches for Monday open their doors every day of the week and not just on Sunday they impact the community they live among. This has worked well for us, and I hope that our ways spark your imagination and that you will discover additional ways to address the 8-to-5 Monday-to-Friday widow. How do you envision your church embedding itself in the marketplace and fostering next-generation creativity?

Whole-life Discipleship

Another of the three main elements of Church for Monday is whole-life discipleship. Whole-life discipleship is not a classroom curriculum that churches teach, but rather a deep-seated seamless faith that believers live everywhere they go. Churches for Monday equip believers with a holistic faith that affects the work they do, commissioning them to Monday's mission field, deploying both their faith in God and their gifts from God.

Whole-life Discipleship and Neighborly Love

If we know that God has called us to love our neighborhoods by seeking peace and prosperity, how then should we do it? It is possible for a church to pursue the thriving of its own city by lifting it economically. But, to significantly affect a place, the church needs to spend a significant amount of time there. Some churches do occasional good works in their communities. Others do event-based outreach; however, most do not stay long enough to see substantial community transformation. Most event-based good works do not have a lasting impact because the church does not become an integral part of its neighborhoods. The church enters the life of its community for a brief moment and then it exits back to the margins of society—within its safe walls.

If we want people to make life-changing decisions at our place of worship without us doing life at their place of work, it's like doing a high dive before learning to swim. It simply doesn't happen that way, because disciple-making must begin at our city's "Jerusalem," the marketplace.

As pastors and church leaders, we have our work cut out for us. We need to equip our congregations for whole-life discipleship to integrate faith and work. Although there is a burgeoning conversation across the country about faith integration, there is still a big disconnect between what we do on Sunday and how we prepare people to go to work on Monday. Lots of churches do a lot of good things but often these good things are focused on the minority of time, not the majority of time of where the believers spend their days.

To prepare believers for whole-life discipleship, pastors can take several equipping steps:

- Preach sermons that lead individuals to worship in every area of their lives.

- Avoid dichotomized vocabulary.

- Teach that what is not sinful is sacred.

- Remind believers that God establishes the works of our hands, so to do meaningful work is virtuous (Ps. 90:17).

- Show that church work is not higher than marketplace work; it is a different vocational call, and all calling, in the church or in the marketplace is to glorify God.

- Commission believers to missional living through their vocations wherever they take them.

- Pray for the industries the congregants enter every day at work—their mission field.

- Establish a leadership pipeline that deploys leaders in every sector of society, not just in religion.

- Foster next-generation creativity and innovation.

• Facilitate economic impact.

These are a few ways that pastors can bridge the Sunday-to-Monday gap. Some may find them a breath of fresh air, and some may look at this list as utterly overwhelming. Pastors are rarely equipped to understand their congregants' industries or the challenges in the economy. The majority are not entrepreneurs so they feel ill-prepared to equip others in what they do not understand. That is a fair concern. What to do?

Pastors, we can take a deep breath. God hasn't tasked us to be the persons with knowledge in all spheres of life. We only need to be the conveners of people who have the knowledge and practice in the things the church needs to be trained. A single individual is not intended to do all the equipping in the church. That is why God gave us the different offices of service. The church is a team, although often it doesn't feel this way. For greater missional impact, it's time for both pastors and congregants to break the stereotype and encourage each other so we can all have our hands on the plow. If pastors start convening a team of people with different spiritual gifts and skills to thoughtfully consider how to accomplish the mission of the church, the load will be lightened.

To help you envision and lead marketplace endeavors, invite people from your church and from the community to join in a "Discovery and Conversation." You, your team, and the Holy Spirit can come up with great solutions in your community. Look for business savvy people just as you look for Bible savvy people to lead a Bible study. Bringing entrepreneurs, accountants, corporate managers, chefs, construction foremen, artists and the like together will affirm their vocational calling and utilize their Spirit-empowered strengths for the betterment of the community. The church is God's primary tool of redemption. Let's unleash whole-life disciples for optimum influence inside and outside its walls.

Translating the Gospel for a Postmodern, Post-Christian, Post-truth Culture

The third main element of Church for Monday is gospel-translating. The beauty of the gospel message is in the restoration of the brokenness. There is so much chaos in this world that anytime we can model God's restorative order we translate for cultural illegibility the work of Christ and His love for humanity.

Truth in a postmodern, post-Christian, post-truth society is primarily tribal. People are skeptical of overarching truth, but if we can engage them in an experiential truth of Jesus' restorative work in their own social groups, or at their own place of work, school, or family that is what convinces most, and especially the Millennials and the Gen Zs. To accomplish the call of repentance and reconciliation, Churches for Monday present the gospel in a culturally accessible way so people can understand where they have missed it.

Who Are We Translating the Gospel To?

The gospel translated is our *what*. Yet, to contextualize for cultural illegibility, we need to decide also on *who* and *how*. Here is a question to help us decide that: *Who* are we translating the gospel to? To paraphrase: "Who is our target audience?" If we desire to be a community-flourishing church, then we need to re-discover our apostolic commission by examining to whom we are sent. Often we answer the above question naively by saying that we, as a local church, are sent to all people. The truth is we have limited capacity and won't be able to reach everyone in our city, state, country, and the world. So, understanding our target of compassion and our capacity is essential to fulfilling our mission.

Two realities have helped me wrestle with the question of *who* my church and I are sent to reach. First, I had to humbly admit the obvious, that to be human is to be limited. There is freedom in this admission. God is not surprised, or displeased, by our limited ability to serve our spheres of influence. All He is looking for is that we will be fruitful by being faithful in the areas He has called us to multiply kingdom value for His name-sake (Matt. 25:14—30).

Second, there are other harvest workers in the field. I know Jesus exhorted us to pray for more workers, I do that often, but you and I are not the only ones getting the work done. Several years ago, while approaching burnout, I had to concede our local church was not the only one God has stirred with compassion and given the capacity to provide for the particular demographics we desired to help. Learning to embrace both my limitations and my brothers and sisters from other local churches and denominations that are beating with the same heartbeat as ours has been a liberating experience. To say I have mastered letting go of peripheral tasks to focus on the ones we are uniquely positioned and resourced to do, would be an overstatement. Nevertheless, I'm willingly growing in discernment, better recognizing what's ours to do, and able to release what's another's, in order to walk a path of unhurried shalom in the midst of intense demands.

Friends, my prayer for you as you read *Church for Monday* is that you don't walk away overwhelmed by how much there is to do, but you walk away excited for what's there for you to do and also liberated that you are called to do only the things you and your congregation are equipped and positioned to do. I pray you are able to leave the rest for another pastor and another local church to do.

So now that you can catch your breath because you know there is work that is not designed for your plate, you might be asking yourself what are some effective ways to discover *who* you are sent to—your target demographics—in order to discover the problems they have and then support those people in finding meaningful solutions.

First Step

There is an obvious step to get us on the way of our target audience: prayer. Prayer is your first step because the Holy Spirit is the best guide toward the people He has prepared the local church to reach. Especially pay attention to the stirrings in your heart, "for it is God who works in you to will and to act in order to fulfill his good purpose" (Phil. 2:13). The strong desires you and your congregation have to right particular issues, injustices or brokenness in your community might be God at work in you. As you pray and seek ways to be a helpful partner in your community, look for opportunities so God can work through you.

Next Steps in Discovering Your Target Demographics

Pastors may feel awkward asking, "*Who* is our target audience? *Who* does our church want to reach?" It feels limiting. Yet, the reality is, if a church takes time to discover where God has positioned them and how their passions and heart's desires address the problems around them, they will have discovered the work the Holy Spirit has prepared them to do.

To get a better insight on how to define the people we are sent to—our target audience—I interviewed Gabbie Bradford, [3] a digital marketing expert that has over eight years of experience at leading agencies in the industry and is a whole-life disciple in the marketplace. This is what she had to say:

"If you start to look at your church through the lens of a business, you realize that your resources (money and time) are finite. But you've been entrusted to reach people for Christ and, therefore, it's important to figure out the best way to use your resources to connect with your community effectively.

The difference between a business and a church is a business first creates a product and then goes to the target audience. However, for the church, it is the reverse because you're already planted in a particular location. So, you want to reverse engineer to discover who resides in your community. By creating an environment that's reflective of your community, you have the best chance to convey God's message because then the people will be receptive and feel that they belong. They will see you've taken the time to understand them and create a space reflecting their unique personality and needs — where they can truly be themselves and connect with God.

If you're still not sure where to start looking for those you are sent to, the best way is to go outside and start exploring. Do some "market research" in your area. If this were a business, you could conduct surveys and leverage social media to better understand your customer. The same can apply to a church. The "research" is as simple as exploring local places where people hang out, do commerce, and where they frequent every day. Does your neighborhood have a coffee shop where different groups gather daily? Maybe your local college has a big influence on the types of businesses that spring up? Understand the types of people that reside in your area either by people watching and observing your surroundings, or striking up conversations.

Another great tool for mining insights in your community is social media. You can conduct "social listening" on platforms like

Instagram, Twitter, Facebook, and Next Door. For Instagram and Twitter, you can conduct relevant keyword, hashtag and geo-location searches to understand what your local community is thinking, engaging with, and what they truly care about. You can also understand their grievances too, which is a great way to address their concerns and help provide solutions that will benefit the community.

For example, maybe you see that many people are upset with the fact that there are no coffee shops open on Sundays and they want a place to gather or catch up on some work. Why not solve that problem and offer the church as a place to gather on Sunday afternoons where people can have a book club or work on their side business? Maybe you notice your local elementary school is running low on funds for after school activities. Your church can offer an after school program or a scholarship fundraiser to help alleviate that need. Social listening provides valuable insights into the community God has placed us in to care for. Social listening is also a great way to make sure you're connecting with a group of people you may be struggling to understand. If you really want to grow your young adult group at church, why not understand what they're sharing on social media. Not only will you learn their favorite movies, music, and TV shows, but you'll understand what they're struggling with most. People are sometimes more open and vulnerable on their Instagram accounts than in real life. Maybe you see that many young adults are struggling with anxiety and juggling the pressures of school, friends, and social media. That could be a topic you tackle in the next sermon series or in the young adult class. It's important to offer relevant information that will help connect and impact their lives, and one of the best ways to understand what they need is by listening (especially on social media).

Speaking of social media, you can't ignore Facebook groups, one of the fastest-growing parts of the Facebook platform. Here, people are still very actively posting and sharing with one another, and odds are your local community has several local Facebook groups you can request to join. These groups usually have a theme (business, housing, interest-based, etc.), so find a few and go through the posts to figure out what your community is talking about and then prayerfully consider which segment of your community your church is positioned to do life with.

An app to try is called Next Door. This is a local social networking app that lets you join a group of people who live in your neighborhood. People share a variety of topics in their neighborhood channel (housing, work opportunities, crime, complaints, garage sales, etc.). It's a great way to understand at a very local level what is happening and also connect with people who literally live next door to your church.

Once you have an understanding of who your local community is comprised of, start to think of ways to tailor your church experience for them. Perhaps you start several different small groups for the subsets of people in your community. Stay at home moms may want to meet in the mid-mornings (and you can offer free childcare) versus working professionals who might want to meet in the evenings (offer them networking opportunities). If you figure out that your community has a big passion for its local football team, why not host a tailgate or hang a banner outside that cheers them on game day. Finding ways to incorporate your community into your programs, décor, and traditions will go a long way in establishing the church as a part of the community rather than outside of it.

You can take it a step further by starting to engage in conversations with your community not only in person but as a church online as well. Social media is a powerful communication tool and you can establish a voice for your church and reach people that may not be comfortable coming through the church doors. As you're conducting your social listening campaign you can start conversations with people where you will begin an open dialog and start to establish a real relationship. You might chat with someone through social media for several months before they feel compelled to even step foot into your church, but they'll finally want to take that step after you've taken the time to cultivate the relationship online first. Think of social media as an extension of the church and not only use it as a way to promote the church but also a means to build one-on-one relationships with people in your community.

This isn't a linear process, it's cyclical. We should always be in "discovery mode"—actively listening and learning new things about our communities. In this way, we'll be able to evolve our church's offerings and programs to keep up with the community's interests and needs. It's not about changing the Word to fit the community. Rather it's about creating a relevant space to invite the community in so they have an open mind and heart to hear the message. We're never going to get them to be open to the gospel without us first putting in the work to give them a place and experience where they feel accepted.

This parallels what you'd do from a business perspective, where you want to provide value to your customers before asking them for a sale. So, if you're selling juice, you may provide educational videos about superfood ingredients, or create funny memes about kale, or share inspirational quotes to keep them motivated on their wellness journey. You'll have to give to your consumers first many times, gain their trust and develop a relationship before you even think about asking them to buy your juice. Then, when you're asking for their business, they'll jump at the chance because this is a brand that really understands them and a brand they trust. Same goes for the church—we need to give before we ask them to receive the message."

How Will We Translate the Gospel to Our Target Audience?

After we have discerned *who* God has placed us among and sent us to, we need to decide *how* we want to reach them. We'll discuss that in more detail in the following chapters as we discuss the Sunday-to-Monday connect bridge, the integration onramps, and see examples of churches doing this successfully.

Churches for Monday must keep in mind our methodologies provide an incarnational presence, as we manifest love in selfless action for the common good without ostracizing the community's weakness, but instead helping the hurting experience foretastes of King Jesus' shalom (Heb. 4:14-16). Under these circumstances, it is likely that our targeted unchurched audience will listen more willingly to the salvation message because we will show them we truly care and have taken their uniqueness to heart.

Other Characteristics of Church for Monday

In addition to the three main components, there are additional elements that characterize, in varying degrees, Churches for Monday. They are the dual usage of their church property; having high-touch, experience-based, and Spirit-evident environments; primarily growing from conversions, not transfers, and often being led by co-vocational pastors. Such churches are flourishing and as a result, the communities God placed them within are flourishing, too.

Dual Usage of Church Property

Church facilities are more than just buildings. Our church campuses send a message about what is important to us. They answer questions like, "Can I check your place out if I'm not coming on Sunday?" or "Do you care about my life events and make room for me on your property?"

We can prosper the community and increase the sustainability of our churches if we are open to innovative ways of utilizing our properties. Finding creative revenue streams to fund the church's vision and accelerate generosity is important when supplementing the congregants' tithes and offerings. What if pastors serve their communities by renting out building space that stays empty most of the week for entrepreneurial training, holiday events, birthday parties, continuing education programs, corporate retreats or office use? At Real Life, renting our facility for community usage provides us a way to care for the unchurched and bring a life-line revenue to our, otherwise, scarce, church-planting budget. In doing so we also create familiarity with people who would never step inside our buildings. It is a win-win situation: reaching new demographics *and* generating funds for more missional work. Pastors may feel that strategizing about "making money" taints their mission, but just like a business, a church requires fiscal viability to carry out transformational activities.

High-touch, Experience-based, and Spirit-evident

The way I see it, the future of the church will be high-touch, experience-based, and Spirit-evident because, although we live in a high-tech connected world, we are relationally isolated. And yet,

God created us for community and there is real yearning for genuine friendships. We see this hunger evident in the tribal cultures that have emerged in social media, politics, and even sports. In addition, people around us are looking for the spiritual although not necessarily seeking it in the Christian church.

What if we were to once again reclaim the supernatural as our hallmark? The reductionism of the gospel, about which we'll talk in the following pages, has pushed the church toward explanation and defense of our faith but the reality is that we cannot explain everything about God through our reason. What if the supernatural were to once again be our high-touch? Our post-truth neighbor is not looking for more facts but more experience. The gospel message needs to touch people's hearts not just their ears. Making room for the Holy Spirit's revelation gives us a way to better connect to an experience-oriented culture. Here are a few ideas to facilitate authentic, high-touch, Spirit-evident environments.

- Pastors can include Q & A's in their sermons to better engage the listener.

- The worship services can occasionally, or on regular basis, offer breakfast, lunch, or dinner with testimony segments to gel the community in one family by eating together and getting to know the stories of many in the church.

- Teach Bible studies that allow for faith exploration and sharing.

- Facilitate hands-on workshops.

- Offer goal-setting vision boards to invite the community to explore God's direction in their lives.

These are some of our ways to build genuine community. What are your ways?

Conversion-based, Not Transfers

In a society that is overwhelmed with information and looks for more experience not more knowledge, being genuinely changed not just informed about a godly lifestyle will make the pivotal difference of who sticks around a community of believers. Add to this the continuous unfavorable treatment of Christians in our society, it can be anticipated that when local churches grow they will grow through conversions, not transfers.

Co-Vocational Pastors

The co-vocational lens helps us tear down the sacred and secular divide. It affirms all callings as having kingdom value, worth, and dignity. In this respect, all work we do is worship unto God and can be seen as "full-time ministry" done in different settings.

Pastors, often because of necessity, have worked two jobs—one at church and one in the marketplace. But as the church can bring them on full-time salary they drop the marketplace job. This is what we know as bi-vocational.

Now, there is a rise in a different trend: co-vocational pastors. The co-vocational pastors differ from the bi-vocational in this—their two vocations are aligned within one calling and one life purpose focused on Jesus' kingdom. The co-vocational pastor doesn't keep a secular job just to pay the bills and looks at it as a necessary secular evil in order to fulfill the true calling of the sacred. Neither is counting the days for when there are enough finances from the church to pay for a full employment salary so the outside job can go away. [4] Instead, he or she sees the value of being personally embedded in the economy to interact with and reach to the culture outside of a Christian workplace.

I have chosen the route of co-vocational pastor by working as a business consultant and a lead pastor. This has been a good choice for me and for the church as I keep in close relationship with the business community for whom our church is passionate to reach. Church for Monday pastors often opt for co-vocation to exemplify the main characteristics of these churches: whole-life disciples who are gospel-translating and embedded in the economy. Is there a segment in the marketplace that your church is passionate to make a difference in and where you can enter to work, even in a part-time capacity to help you keep your finger on the pulse of the people you care for?

Flourishing Communities

Because Churches for Monday see themselves as spiritual and economic engines of their communities, the places in which they serve flourish. By being embedded in the marketplace, the whole-life disciples translate the gospel and fulfill their call to be the contemporary incarnate witness for a holy God who desires *shalom* for all communities.

Churches that desire to equip for work become cultural anthropologists attuned to what is going on in the community, strategizing with the Holy Spirit toward inspired futures. Will you join this growing number of churches who are loving their communities into economic and social lift? When we do this the community will likely see our churches as an attentive and authentic neighbor thereby open their hearts to experience the full shalom of our Lord, welcome him as Savior, and experience holistic lift.

A Real-Life Story — Church for Monday Integrating Faith into the Marketplace

Corner Church in Minneapolis, Minnesota, calls people to be redefiners as they seek to represent Christ clearly in community. Pastor Scott Woller knows the church culture where invitation and information are foundational elements to evangelism. In this culture, pastors task their parishioners with inviting everyone to come to church gatherings where they will receive all the pertinent information about Jesus and be invited to be saved. Woller doesn't find this strategy to be as effective as it used to be in the past because, as he explains, people now have a very different view of the church. Here is what he describes as the thoughts he now assumes someone has when he invites them to church:

"Are you inviting me to your mindless, manipulative, abusive, hateful, right-wing, sexist, and bigoted group?"

"Are you thinking your little presentation will change my opinion of you and make me want to become one of you?"

"You say you love me, but you only want to count me as a religious victory."

Woller poses the question we all are asking: How can this distorted definition of church and Christians be changed? When a person has a bad experience at a restaurant, what does it take for him or her to go back? It takes more than an invitation and a promise that things have changed. Re-entry requires a redefinition built in a new reality. In 2006, Scott and Amber Woller planted Corner Church with the vision of having a Corner Church and a valued-in-the-community business within walking distance of everyone in the urban dense communities in Minneapolis. Today, Corner Church is in three communities with three community coffee shops. The coffee shops, Corner Coffee, are local, independent coffee houses focused on adding value to the community. While the coffee shops are not run as Christian or church coffee shops, they are closed on Sundays, and all Corner Church services are held in the coffeehouse spaces. Having a community-focused business with a frequent and localized customer base is not simply about economic viability, it is missional as well. Rather than sitting inside a church building waiting for members of the community to come in, Corner Church has placed itself in the middle of the community. This intentional placement fosters relationships and, in turn, redefinition.

While there is organizational intentionality, relationship still comes out of people loving people. Corner Church encourages and empowers the church body to love their most local community first and to prioritize love for family, friends, neighbors, and coworkers. Corner Church calls the body to meet their local community's needs early by not focusing on being a hero when the situation becomes dire, but rather they focus on building meaningful relationships long before a superhero is needed. Lastly, Corner Church advocates for doing this love and investment together. The Apostle Paul challenged Christ's followers to see personal value while realizing we are incomplete and we leave others incomplete when we function alone.

Corner Church services deliberately seek to be an environment for redefinition as well. Rather than seeing pastoral teaching as a moment to simply tell people what to think, believe, and do, it is a moment to invite people into the process of being refined by Christ. This is done by bringing coaching principles and teaching into pastoral presentations. This results in sermons where teaching is punctuated by three or four intentional dialogue questions where tables of people are tasked with processing the content being presented. This process is messy but essential in moving from poor definitions of Christ and church, such as those without heart or practice, to pure definitions of Christ and church, where love is practical.

Having a church in multiple communities that owns and operates multiple coffeehouses may sound glamorous, but in reality, it is incredibly arduous and risky. Planting a healthy church or starting a viable small business calls for endless miracles. Doing them together, apart from a clear calling of God, will end painfully and most likely abruptly. The call of God on Corner Church to keep planting in order to keep redefining, pulls them onward."

Pastor Woller encourages us that redefining is not just about Sundays, but it is lived out every day of the week. In what way are you and your church redefiners as you seek to represent Christ clearly in your community?

Chart the Path Forward

Go for Contact

If we envision a new "there," we need to also envision a new pathway to it.

"Here" is where the church bubble is or, the so-called, sacred land.

"There" is where the secular marketplace bubble is and what most think of as the sinful land.

Admittedly, there are churches that have intentionally worked toward integrating faith into the marketplace and are successfully getting "there." However, there are still well-meaning churches that are careful not to touch the secular marketplace bubble, either for lack of clarity or lack of training.

If this conversation about faith into the marketplace is new to you and you find yourself wondering how to do that integration, welcome to the club. Grab a cup of coffee and let's sit down together and chart the path forward. Most of us who practice holistic faith have started where you are and have slowly grown to understand how to live out our faith in the public arena. My hope is that I'll offer you and your church some valuable tools to build integrated ministries and to give you sufficient theological validity for a Church for Monday. If you are reading this book, I trust you are as passionate as I am about the ministry of reconciliation. As you will agree, staying in isolation in our church bubble will not do it. We must "go" to faithfully communicate the gospel.

The Sunday-to-Monday Connect Bridge

To chart a path forward we need to build a Sunday-to-Monday Connect Bridge and Integration Onramps. If we are to connect successfully and go from "here" to "there," local churches have to construct Sunday-to-Monday connect bridges that both Christians and non-Christians can travel on back and forth with ease.

Sunday-to-Monday Connect Bridges are thoughtfully-crafted, biblically-informed, friendly environments that provide foretastes of the kingdom of God to the seekers, skeptics, and nones.

We are not looking to convert people the very first time we shake hands with them. A bridge that is open for connections is open for conversations with seekers and skeptics alike. It is thoughtfully constructed so the unchurched can interact with believers outside of the Sunday morning gathering and explore faith in Christ without being bullied into grace, ostracized for their behavior, or given a list of life's "does" and "don'ts." Remember that we were once "them" and cringed when we were yelled at, pointed at, or picketed. In a society where reasonable discourse has been thrown out of the window, the local church can model a better way of searching for meaningful solutions for our communities' common good.

I'm encouraged many churches now choose to build a Sunday-to-Monday connect bridge as a permanent ministry link between the church and the marketplace, laying its foundation in the patient expectation that those who frequent the bridge will eventually experience the salvific grace of God. I'm not advocating a naïve hope for community engagement and more busy work for the church staff, but instead, a long-term, sincere effort on behalf of all the congregants, both as a scattered and a gathered community, to bring social, economic, and spiritual change right where they do life the majority of their week— at work, at school, and at play in their community.

The Sunday-to-Monday connect bridge is probably one of the most important works that a local church does to integrate faith into the marketplace. Like a bridge that spans the lands that couldn't be traveled before because there was no way to unify them—often crossing over deep waters and impassable ravines—this bridge that the local church builds connects the unchurched to God and brings

God's kingdom at hand with tangible outcomes of his redemption in real geography and time. These outcomes look like foretastes of the kingdom to come. They shape places that practice biblically-faithful justice, mercy, and love; they provide opportunities for creative work that affirms human dignity and diversity by honoring the contributions of women and men of all colors and ethnicities without politicizing the beauty of God's transforming reality.

It will serve us well to remember that connect doesn't mean convert. Sometimes people sense the grace of God in such a compelling way they make a decision to follow Jesus as soon as we engage them. But often that is not the case. Going for contact is not going for proselytizing, but for connecting and convening the grace of God for the common good.

Building a Sunday-to-Monday Connect Bridge

Here are few examples of how the church, both as a scattered and gathered community, can build a Sunday-to-Monday connect bridge to the marketplace and offer valuable resources that lift people socially, economically and spiritually. If a changing job market or high unemployment is the reality of your community, then reaching to the local chamber of commerce, or your public officials, to understand in what ways you can assist them with developing jobs can be a good start. Job-training, job re-training, or entrepreneurial workshops can connect you to the people in your city. As we already discussed, the church doesn't have to be the expert to teach these workshops but can convene the experts and provide or find adequate space. Often we can find HR experts, business owners, leadership development coaches, and consultants right in our own congregations who may not have been a fit to lead a Bible study but are yearning to use their talents for God in a practical way.

If your community is leisure-oriented then community dinners, concerts, and clean comedy shows will provide great contact and a way to engage the arts and entertainment sphere. You can partner with other wholesome entities in your city and just provide space, dinner, or volunteers. Being present in a meaningful way to do life with people in your city is a valuable first step in establishing lasting social capital. Also, if your community experiences racial, gender, ethnic or other tensions you may offer safe environments for round-table discussions done in respectful ways at your neutral place.

In your community, there are many opportunities for building Sunday-to-Monday connect bridges that will set your church on a successful trajectory to build social capital and impact the public arena. Every community has its unique challenges, and the local churches Jesus is building amidst their marketplace are uniquely positioned to bring wise, Spirit-inspired solutions for holistic restoration.

Regardless of the specifics, the goal of the Sunday-to-Monday connect bridge is to provide friendly environments, without being "preachy" in feel and expression. This type of church-to-marketplace outreach will span far when overcoming the sacred/secular divide. Being present with our communities to develop lasting relationships is an essential first step to regain a respected seat at the table.

Integration Onramps

By building a Sunday-to-Monday Connect Bridge the church ushers in the restorative presence of God in the marketplace. The Sunday-to-Monday Connect Bridge has Integration Onramps both for people who are skeptical observers of faith, agnostics, or nones—and for Christians who want to know how to close the Sunday-to-Monday gap between faith, work, and economics. Unless we have integration onramps to help us get from the church bubble to the bridge or from the marketplace bubble to the bridge, the bridge itself will be useless.

From Dichotomized to Integrated Onramps

In order to go from dichotomized faith (bubble living) to integrated faith (bridge living), pastors are called to lead in abolishing the divide when it comes to calling and vocation and then to model whole-life discipleship in his or her own pastoral practice. Here are some ways church leaders can build integration onramps for bridge living:

- Language

One of the first things to do when desiring to shift culture and go from "here" to "there" is to change our language because language conveys culture. We have to ask ourselves: "What are we saying with the words we choose to use?" In order to prepare your church for greater impact on Monday, you need to make a communication shift. Shift to a seamless, biblically faithful, and integral language. If, when talking about God's calling on people's lives, we only talk about full time ministry in Christian vocations and emphasize only those who are called in the 501(c)3 world such as missionaries at home or abroad, pastors, full time church clergy and staff, workers with human trafficking, or counselors for people affected by the opioid crisis, we communicate that these are the God-chosen and blessed vocations. Without a doubt, all these are excellent vocations, but we often commission these vocations without recognizing publically the redemptive value of the for-profit vocations in the secular sector. What about the truck driver, the mechanic, the office manager, and the Wall-Street Banker? We also perpetuate the division when we talk about:

Eternal vs. temporal

Material vs. spiritual

Sacred vs. secular

If this is the first time you are considering the implications of this divided view of God and his redemptive work in the world, the conversation may cause you to pause and take a deep breath. There are excellent resources one can glean from, such as The Made to Flourish network, [1] which offers a plethora of sound teachings on these topics, as well as Theology of Work. [2]

Pastoral Workplace Visits

The pastor can start visiting his or her congregants at work. Many churches around the country have adopted this as part of the pastoral routine. A pastor friend of mine who leads a large, multi-campus church says workplace visits are as important to him as hospital visits. He faithfully does both.

When pastors build into their weekly schedules this vital function of shepherding—workplace visits—it allows them to connect the two worlds, the church, and the marketplace, and to assume the place of a learner, not just a teacher. This way they can understand work issues better, connect with their people at a deeper level, convey to the congregants: "Your work matters to God," and build an onramp for Christians to connect their faith to their work.

• Celebrate Monday Calling on Sunday

As part of the service flow or liturgy, we can celebrate Monday calling during the Sunday service. This can be done in many ways and pastors can be as creative as their church format allows them to be.

One way we do it at Real Life Church is to have once a month a service centered on a common meal and a sermon based on testimony interviews. I invite three persons in front, one at a time. The person and I sit instead of stand for a casual interview-style talk. I ask guiding questions and the interviewee shares how God is faithful in their work-life during the month and how God's grace leads them to make wise choices in different areas of life: at work, at school, at play and at home.

Different churches around the country are doing similar Monday celebrations on Sunday. To shape your church's culture, you can name them creatively such as Monday on Sunday, Biz Chats, Monday Times, or This Time Tomorrow. The pastors can ask questions to keep the interview focused on the Monday mission we want to celebrate on Sunday. Here are three suggested questions:

1. Tell us what has God called you to do this time tomorrow?

2. What are the joys and challenges to be a follower of Jesus where God has called you?

3. How can we pray for you?

When the pastor prays at the end for the person interviewed, he or she can stand up, extend their hand and commission this person to their calling and also others in the congregation who might be engaged in the same type of work. This set apart time on Sunday to highlight what people do on Monday shows them your church really knows the world of your congregation and God cares about their vocation.

• Commissioning Non-Pastoral Professions

People often sit in our church pews for decades before they see someone like themselves on stage doing similar professions as their own and being highlighted as to how God moves in their life and their work. To equip our people to integrate faith at work, it is essential for pastors to show them God blesses the work of their hands (Ps. 90:17). If you've never commissioned people to their vocations, here are a few thoughts on how you can begin.

Labor Day is a natural time to celebrate the work our congregants do and the priesthood of all believers. The pastor can preach on the importance of calling and work and do commissioning for work. Because this is a national holiday celebrating work on this day might be an easy starting point for your church.

Teachers can be commissioned in the fall when the school year begins.

Monthly Commissioning can happen during the prayer time of the segment "Celebrate Monday Calling on Sunday". Churches that do this on regular basis have the opportunity to highlight different vocations with paid and unpaid work because the church features retirees, students, stay at home moms and dads, alongside CEOs, plumbers, accountants, and baristas.

• Forming a Richer Business and Entrepreneurial Appreciation and Vocabulary

Often pastors are open to cheering their congregants in their vocations but they would like to become better versed in the tensions that exist in the business world and to master the language of business and entrepreneurship. Reading business books and magazines such as *Wall Street Journal* or the *Entrepreneur Magazine* will give the pastor an expanded understanding about the lives many in his or her congregation live at work.

• Asset Mapping of Congregants

Every individual we pastor has a sphere of influence and potential contributions they can make to the community and the marketplace. In order to get more familiar with the specifics of the congregant's work, the pastor can ask what articles or books they recommend for good insights about their field of work.

Allowing the Spirit to Lead.

While building the Sunday-to-Monday Connect Bridge and the Integration Onramps the church's goal is to discern where to join God in his mission in the community. The fact is we don't take God into the city. His Spirit is already at work there and beckons the church to partner with God so He can work through His church for the life of His world. How can we perceive where to join God at work? Here are some ways our churches can invite the Holy Spirit to lead.

~ Prayer

~ Assessment of gifts and skills of the local church.

~ Assessment of your community's strengths and skills.

~ Assessment of the restlessness of your community.

~ Answer questions the community is asking.

Often we sponsor events hoping for a marketplace engagement, but we don't get it because we haven't done our research to understand what the community is seeking to know, wrestle with, or overcome.

~ The Community's Desire for change (not just need for change)

What I'm talking about is the desire for transformation people have in a particular crisis area in the marketplace. We know change is difficult and people usually don't opt for it unless the present pain exceeds the pain of change. The good news is God is patient with us. He never twists our arm into transformation. Discovering the areas the Spirit is stirring in people's heart to see anew, be healed and transformed takes thoughtful evaluation and deep listening to God and the community.

- The Congregation's Preparedness to help and not just its aspiration to help.

- The Congregation's Desire to get ready in order to act upon the opportunity for redemption.

An Agent of Spiritual, Social, and Economic Transformation

Without capacity, we cannot practice compassion. Often the church does very well in developing biblically-informed compassion, but without resources, we cannot extend that compassion to our neighbors. To be a church which impacts the marketplace on Monday we have to develop both compassion and capacity. We are called to be both faithful and fruitful. For that reason, we have to strategically plan not only to grow attendance, evangelistic outreaches, and small group discipleship, but also job and wealth creation for our congregants, and the people from our community. To do that we must map the church's present capacity. It is crucial to prayerfully plan for the sustainability of the local church so it continues to be a stable, well-managed agent of transformation which remains faithfully present in a community over the long haul.

Pastors can map the church's capacity by doing Asset-Based Community Development (ABCD), a methodology that seeks to uncover and utilize the strengths within communities as a means for sustainable development. It helps communities become stronger and more self-reliant by discovering, mapping, and mobilizing all their local assets instead of just focusing on needs, deficiencies, and problems.

Asset Mapping of individuals, entire congregations, or communities by collecting answers to some of the following questions below gives a great foundation to evaluate the church's and the community's readiness to work toward a mutually flourishing future.

Asset Mapping Assessment

GIFTS, TALENTS, LANGUAGES: What natural and supernatural gifts and talents do you have? Do you speak a foreign language? (e.g., musician, artist, cook, administration, hospitality, help, mechanical ability, technology expert, poetry, public speaking, dancing, energy, passion, compassion, strength, joy, creativity, hard worker, etc)?

SKILLS AND HOBBIES: What skills and hobbies do you have? (e.g., sports, sewing, knitting, embroidering, painting, hiking, skateboarding, biking, etc.?

Are you willing to teach these skills? Yes or No (*circle one*)

MISSIONS & EVANGELISM:
Do you want to be the message of hope in Jesus in a relevant and cultural way?
Joining school partnerships, planning events, media, missions, and evangelism?

ASSIMILATION/ CONGREGATIONAL CARE:
Do you enjoy meeting and getting to know new people?
Is helping others important to you?
Do you enjoy serving and making others feel welcomed and at ease?
Do you enjoy sharing the results of your cooking and baking skills?
When others are in need do you share your practical skills?
Is it important for you to share your concern for others in practical ways?

DISCIPLESHIP:
Do you have a desire and willingness to help facilitate the learning, growing, and maturation of people in all areas of their life? (I.e. finances, work, spiritual disciplines, salvation, relationships, addictions, and hang-ups)

CURRENT OCCUPATION:
RESOURCES: What resources can you offer? What is your formal, professional and educational training? (e.g., nurses, doctors, lawyers, young people, people connected to government, access to relatives at the bank, etc.)?

CORPORATIONS/INSTITUTIONS AND ASSOCIATION/ NETWORKS:
What connections with other groups, agencies or policymakers do

you have? (e.g., your own workplace, Chamber of Commerce, School Board, Rotary Club, Political Party, etc.)?

INTENT: Would you be willing to work together to affect Transformational Development in our community?
Yes or No (*circle one*)

Worship, Work, and Entrepreneurship

By now you may have begun to wonder: "Why is this connection between worship and the workplace so important? Why should an average church in our country affirm and encourage entrepreneurship?" My own experience in reaching and serving entrepreneurs led me to observe firsthand the growing disconnect between faith and the marketplace, and especially among small business owners and the Christian church. Not because entrepreneurs are not looking for spirituality, but often because the Christian spiritual leaders are not making room for them in their congregations. Pastors shy away from preaching about business and the good that it does for our society. Thus, the majority of small business owners remain unchurched and skeptical of the church, thinking that if pastors reach out to them, they are only interested in their money support for the church's projects.

I realize unless you are a church planter you might not be an entrepreneur yourself, but you likely want to affirm the entrepreneurs in your church and in your community. The entrepreneurs around you want that as much as you do. Most of them lead busy, lonely lives because of the nature of their small business enterprises. They crave community and will thrive if your church provides community-building opportunities. Your church can take steps toward connecting with the entrepreneurs in your city by opening your facility for entrepreneurial networking events and business group meetings. Offer coffee and possibly snacks. But most importantly, offer a warm, friendly atmosphere. The entrepreneurs will not look for pastors to preach at these events but to greet and listen. Down the road it is likely pastors will get the opportunity to life-coach his or her new entrepreneur-friends. I pray for your success as you venture into this opportunity to integrate faith and entrepreneurship.

Pastoring a City

I will state the obvious to help us to see beyond it: We are called to pastor the people in a city, not a building in that city. Seeing our call as pastoring the whole city and its marketplace and not just whoever chooses to come on Sunday morning to our property is crucial to thriving communities. It compels us to build Sunday-to-Monday connect bridges and integration onramps because pastoring a city does not just mean addressing the believers in our churches to the neglect of addressing the private and public ills of our communities. Pastoring a city is to care for the entire life of the entire marketplace God has positioned us to impact by creating spiritual, social, and economic value. I am encouraged some of you are already pastoring your cities well and others are making their first steps. Expand your circle wider now and consider how you might serve recent high school grads looking for a career, college students who are working through their degree, young married mothers re-entering the workforce, or singles struggling with loneliness? Who are the people in the marketplace you are prepared to engage and add value to? Be encouraged God has enabled you and your church to usher Jesus' shalom into the crumbling places of your community.

A Real-Life Story — Building a Sunday-to-Monday Connect Bridge

In Mason, Ohio, kingdom-minded and business-oriented pastor Jeff Greer leads a congregation at Grace Chapel church that believes every member has a significant role in advancing the Kingdom of God. He has created an entrepreneurial culture at Grace Chapel, which celebrates and empowers lay leaders to create, what he calls, Biznistries. They are for-profit, self-sustaining enterprises commissioned for a kingdom purpose, operating according to biblical principles, integrating ministry at every level, and releasing a flow of funds for further ministry advances. Here is Grace Chapel's story shared with me by Greer in a written interview.

"Instead of just starting businesses (what we call biznistries) in developing countries we started them at home as well," says Greer. Grace Chapel started an Angel Fund to help generate capital for their start-ups. Some of the Biznistries that the church has launched include the ORCA Center (a co-working space) and CrossFit Superfly (a gym) located on the church's campus. ORCA involves a business accelerator, an incubator, as well as business seminars, training, and team building. There is office space within the ORCA Center for local entrepreneurs with the same heart and passion. A sister venture capital organization, Self-Sustaining Enterprises (SSE), is also hosted on the campus. SSE provides training, coaching, and start-up capital to entrepreneurs launching new Biznistries.

This Ohio church is building a global community of Christ-followers awakening imagination, igniting passion and unleashing purpose. For whether believers are at work, at school or at home, God can use everyone's gifts, talents, and abilities to impact the world. Greer is adamant:

> In a Biblical worldview, things are either sacred or sinful, not secular or sacred. God created everything, Satan created nothing, and dynamic leaders are tired of God being left with a few hours of our time on Sunday and surrendering the rest to the enemy. We must ask ourselves, why we surrender territory to the enemy that doesn't belong to him. Grace Chapel's Marketplace Ministry is one of the largest, most innovative marketplace ministries in the world. At the campus of Grace Chapel in Mason, Ohio, we host individual entrepreneur-owned small businesses, businesses that are integrated with the ministry of the Church.

Greer believes many people have saved what is necessary for their future and are not motivated by money, but they are inspired by a challenge and want to help the defenseless and lost people in the world. Pete is one of those people. Pete retired early from Proctor & Gamble to become the director of SSE. He would say he often works harder now than before he retired. Ibrahim, a chemist, and inventor, originally from Nigeria, has also joined the team and is making an impact through his innovative technology. "We have heard story after story," Greer says, "of people coming alive that were once only marginally engaged in the body of Christ. There are former CFOs, CEOs, attorneys, marketing directors, scientists, and salespeople ready to invest their lives in a Spirit-driven cause. And best of all, they are willing to work for free if they believe in your vision. Pastors, take a moment to dream and ask the question, *"What if?"* What if entrepreneurs and business people saw the Church as a first step in finding solutions to the challenges they face in the marketplace?"

This is a valid point for church leaders to consider. Grace Chapel's story both inspires and challenges us to discover new ways through which our churches can practice effective marketplace integration. How can the church once again become an institution sought for its generosity, loving nature, wisdom, problem-solving, respect, soul care, and spiritual advancement? It is imperative for the future of the church, and the world, for believers to bridge the Sunday-to-Monday worship-to-work gap in order to recover a place of social influence in culture.

PART TWO

CULTURE AND CHURCH

Context, Content, and Consequences of a Post-Modern, Post-Christian, and Post-Truth Society

No More Cushy Greens

When I was in fifth grade, my dad went to work in Mongolia on a government project. My mom and I joined him a year later. I was a curious young girl, fascinated by all the sights, smells and sounds in Darkhan, the second-largest city in the country where my dad worked. I loved to explore its stores with Chinese tea cakes and dazzling deli robes, go to the post office for snail mail from friends and listen to the Asian music spilling from its loudspeakers, and run to the street vendors for the only kind of ice-cream cone in town, a simple vanilla kept in wooden barrels. But most of all, I loved the greens.

In the distance, there was a green expanse that rolled in front of my eyes every morning I woke up and peered through the windows. It looked like a plush velvet carpet, inviting me to do cartwheels on it. I could hardly wait for the end of the workweek when my dad promised to take me to the edge of town, so I could sink my whole body in the cushy green dreamscape. Finally, my dad took me to it. I ran into the grass, unprepared for what I found. My bare feet and my caressing hands got cuts from what turned out to be coarse grass that filled the expanse before me. There was nothing soft about its feel, nothing cartwheel-worthy about its sharp blades, just bleeding hands, feet, and knees. What I expected to be a friendly place turned out to be harsh, hostile grasslands. I thought I knew grass, but all my grass experience was from the soft fields of my own country. I never knew anything like this. This course grass stretched for miles. Once you were in it, there was no end to its pokiness and razor-sharp touches. I wanted to escape as fast as I got in, but it was impossible to move with speed. I ran in with healthy feet, but now, I traversed my way back cautiously and slowly, because I was exiting on bleeding feet. I learned my lesson that day: *study your environment before plunging into it.*

We need to understand our complex postmodern, post-Christian, post-truth society in order to navigate it. Often the church shies away from digging deep into society's trends, philosophy, and structure. Some in the church have the attitude that Scripture is all we need for successful witnessing. In order to share Scripture with our postmodern neighbors, we need to study their postmodern "greens," so we know how to walk the gospel message in their grasslands without having to exit with bleeding feet and no followers.

Studying the postmodern environment in order to understand the culture and translate the gospel message is about living on mission both faithfully and fruitfully. Often, devout Christians put months, if not years, into studying a foreign language and its culture to go as missionaries abroad. Nowadays, the mission field has come to our doorsteps. To speak to it, we must learn the non-churchy language of our post-Christin neighbors, know the beliefs of our postmodern community, and understand our post-truth culture struggles with claims of absolute truths. We cannot translate the gospel in a native language if we do not know that language. The Western society we live in has its own way of communicating. We need to recognize this so our gospel message will not be lost in translation. Let's study our environment, so we can re-imagine how to be a disciple for Monday in our postmodern world.

Context for Postmodernism

The philosophies and the ethics of contemporary Western societies resemble those of the Roman Empire in which the Christian narrative first appeared. Moral decadence, many philosophical options, and religious pluralism mark the prevalent postmodern worldview. [1] Albeit not all people have replaced their modern culture with the postmodern point of view, the postmodern paradigm has taken over mainstream beliefs and has, for the most part, gripped many in the younger generation, thus assuring that the paradigm shift will be complete.

The tenets of postmodernity encourage people toward new religious syntheses. In this new environment, the most pressing spiritual issue is who gets to narrate the world. That is why, unless the contemporary church more fully awakens to the reality in which it exists, it cannot respond effectively to the pagan society. Postmodernism is a term referring to an intellectual mood that calls into question the modern mindset where absolute truth existed. There is a general consensus that postmodernism first appeared in the 1930s but, as a cultural phenomenon, it did not gain momentum until three or four decades later aided by the transition into an information society. [2]

During the 1960s, the mood characterizing postmodernism became attractive to the intellectuals and the artists, who began to offer radical alternatives to the dominant modern culture. In the 1970s, the postmodern challenge further infiltrated the prevailing culture. "Eventually, the adoption of the new teaching became so widespread that the designation "postmodern" crystallized as the overarching label for a diverse social and cultural phenomenon. . . . In the 1980s, the move from fringe to mainstream came to completion . . . it was "cool" to be postmodern." [3] A new historical paradigm had successfully emerged. Now the church faces an urgent Sunday mandate: Equip believers for mission for a new postmodern, post-Christian, post-truth Monday to close the ever-widening cultural Sunday-to-Monday gap.

Autonomy and Choice

From the beginning of human history, all cultural paradigms have used the same core-defining question: "Indeed, did God really say?" (Gen. 3:1).

"Created in the image of God and intended to dominate the earth, man possesses an unbelievably independent and ambitious spirit. It was through pride that he fell, through attempting to free himself from the control of the Creator . . . Above all, he finds it hard to admit his dependence, to recognize the limits of his reason and strength." [4]

Postmodernism pushes the Genesis inquiry to expanded lengths, questions all authority, not just biblical authority. In America there is a palpable distrust of earthly institutions and divine authority—media, government, higher education, and even church. All have suffered in the public opinion. [5]

The postmodern way of thinking carries one of the same core principles as modernity: *autonomy*. Modernism offered humans autonomy from God by unchaining humans from the transcendent; postmodernity takes it a step further and offers autonomy from one another by unchaining humans from any notion of shared human nature. [6]

The roots of this way of thinking are in existentialism, which proclaimed life is absurd, meaningless, and the individual must create his or her own meaning by choices. Postmodernism rejects any notion of universal, overarching truth, and reduces all ideas to social constructions shaped by class, gender, and ethnicity. [7] Indeed, postmodernism views "right answers" with suspicion and equates certainty with dishonesty. In turn, this leads to an individualistic "try before you buy" mentality. Mark Liederback and Alvin L. Reid writes,

> Autonomy is merely disguised behind the idea of communal identity. Devoid of a transcendent basis for moral accountability, the individual simply could choose to leave the given community and find a new one that meets current felt needs or desires. All that would be necessary is learning the language and reinventing oneself in whatever manner one would like. [8]

We see that autonomy trend in the heightened church hopping, declining church attendance, and eroding long-term commitment to a local church. Top-down authority is increasingly rejected, and an entrepreneurial eco-system is becoming the norm in the business sector, where everyone's contribution is welcomed and sought out—and churchgoers are looking for it, too.

These changes may appear daunting to the work of the church, but in some ways are welcomed opportunities, because the new times urge us to re-envision new ways forward. To retool our strategies for assimilation of postmoderns, it will be helpful to consider ways of affirming believers we are united but not uniform. The individual's uniqueness, skills, and gifts are not only desirable but highly valuable, to the whole and to the health of the church. Gone are the days when no one questioned the authority of the Senior Pastor, and he, (very rarely it had been "she"), stood almost on par with God. Now, that title has increasingly been renamed to Lead Pastor, implying there is a team of staff and lay contributors, not just hirelings saying, "Yes, sir" to every command given. As we continue to build on our good foundation from the past, the current culture causes us to be more imaginative when we think what it looks like to prepare the church to translate worship on Sunday to a kingdom witness and foretaste on Monday.

Absolute Truth

Postmodernism denies the possibility of all absolutes, which allows individuals to determine their own private truth in culture. It deems the idea of universal truth to be absurd. [9] Barna Research has conducted several national surveys among different age groups asking if there are moral absolutes and if moral truth is relative to the circumstances. "By a 3-to-1 margin (64% vs. 22%) adults said truth is always relative to the person and their situation. The perspective was even more lopsided among teenagers, 83% of whom said moral truth depends on the circumstances, and only 6% of whom said moral truth is absolute." [10] The surveys also asked people to indicate the basis on which they make their moral and ethical decisions. "By far the most common basis for moral decision-making was doing whatever feels right or comfortable in a situation." [11] Another Barna survey points to 57% of adults and 74%

percent of millennials who agreed strongly or somewhat that "Whatever is right for your life or works best for you is the only truth you can know." [12]

The postmoderns think people who claim to possess absolute truth want to assert power over others, which threatens their desire for autonomy. This attitude, coupled with the Americans' distrust of institutions and the church—only 36 percent strongly believe churches "have their best interest at heart" [13]—presents leaders with a challenge when reimagining sharing the truths of the Bible.

The postmodern relativistic pluralism also seeks to give place to the "local" nature of truth. [14] Postmodern truth is relative to the community in which a person participates. Along these lines, Charles Colson and Nancy Pearcey comment,

> It was a small step from existentialism to postmodernism, in which even the self is dissolved into the interplay of the forces of race, class, and gender. Multiculturalism is not about appreciating folk cultures; it's about the dissolution of the individual into the tribal group. In postmodernism, there is no objective, universal truth; there is only the perspective of the group, whatever the group may be. [15]

To the postmodernist, absolute truth is a fable; truth is not found but created within the community. Since there are many human communities, there are necessarily many different truths that can exist alongside one another. [16] Finally, postmoderns also look beyond reason to non-rational ways of knowing, through other channels such as emotional and intuition. [17]

In our post-truth society, the church will do well to keep all of that in mind as we evaluate the techniques we have been using to reach the unchurched. We still favor apologetics, but its effectiveness has diminished. It is time to realize listening is as potent of a kingdom tool as telling. In a very loud, polarized world, we need to recover the lost art of listening if we are to affect our post-Christian, post-truth neighbors; engaging them in conversations and inviting them, in community, to experience the Creator of truth, instead of simply announcing truth. God is not intimidated that postmodernists want to co-create truth in community. Jesus does this brilliantly as He welcomes us to co-create beautiful futures with

God. Listening to our postmodern neighbors, in order to invite them on a co-creation journey with God is a tool we need to put in our Monday-toolbox, in order to close the Sunday-to-Monday gap.

Pragmatism

Although this new worldview has penetrated all contemporary spheres of life, the majority of people carry on as if not noticing the change. Pragmatism rules. If something works for them, they easily accept it. Postmodernists have adopted a pluralistic view of knowledge and have demonstrated a willingness to allow competing and seemingly conflicting constructions to exist side by side. [18] For example, the point of issue for them is not, "is the proposition or theory correct?' Rather, they want to know 'What does it do?' or 'What is its outcome?'" [19]

Tolerance

Setting norms to all human communities, should apply to moral and spiritual truths. However, contemporary society scoffs at anyone who tries to assert public truth, labeling them as arrogant and intolerant. Of course, with this very assertion, postmoderns self-contradict. They reject absolutes, but they impose relativism and tolerance as the new absolutes. The paradox is, tolerance rules and no exception is tolerated. Without certainty about transcendent truths, or shared morality, postmodernity promotes tolerance as the supreme virtue, and conviction becomes a vice.[20] Postmodernists elevate choice to the ultimate value, the only justification for any action. [21]

A worrisome fact emerges: Christians have widely adopted the postmodern moral relativism; thus, their behavior as "witnesses and foretaste" of another kingdom has been rendered ineffective. The Barna researchers found few Americans turn to their faith as the primary guide for their moral and ethical decisions. The data reveals substantial numbers of Christians approve of the following activities as morally acceptable: abortion, gay sex, sexual fantasies, cohabitation, drunkenness, and viewing pornography. [22] With great concern, the Barna Group cautions believers:

Without some firm and compelling basis for suggesting that such acts are inappropriate, people are left with philosophies such as "if it feels good, do it," "everyone else is doing it" or "as long as it doesn't hurt anyone else, it's permissible." In fact, the alarmingly fast decline of moral foundations among our young people has culminated in a one-word worldview: "whatever." The result is a mentality that esteems pluralism, relativism, tolerance, and diversity without critical reflection of the implications of particular views and actions. [23]

Religious Pluralism

The post-Christian culture has begun to assemble personal faith systems. It makes its own blend of religions from a dozen or more ingredients, including Christianity. Many accept the New Age movement as a fact of life, and karma has become a part of ordinary speech. [24] The Pew Research Center surveyed more than 4,700 U.S. adults and found that in the U.S. belief in a deity is common even among the religiously unaffiliated—a group composed of those who identify themselves, religiously, as atheist, agnostic or "nothing in particular," and are sometimes referred to, collectively, as religious "nones." Nearly three-quarters of religious "nones" (72 percent) believe in a higher power of some kind, even if not in God as described in the Bible. One-third of Americans say they do not believe in the God of the Bible, but that they do believe there is some other higher power, or spiritual force, in the universe. It is a sobering reality in our culture, only a slim majority of Americans (56 percent) say they believe in God "as described in the Bible," yet only one-in-ten do not believe in any higher power or spiritual force. [25]

In my role as CEO at Real Life Center for Entrepreneurial and Leadership Excellence, I am often invited to business meetings with other entrepreneurs where the hunger for spirituality among the unchurched is real, because they are looking for peace and balance amidst the stress of leading their enterprises. Some of them remember the mystical and the supernatural they have experienced in the church of their childhood. Now, they desire to recreate it in their own worlds and in their own ways. So, practices such as channeling and meditation are commonplace, having replaced prayer; tarot cards are drawn for guidance in lieu of the prophetic wisdom of the Holy Spirit. Christian pastors have become unpopular. In place of Christian pastors, the spiritual guides of postmodernism have become the spiritual coach, the healer, and the mystic. This transfer of spiritual leadership is no surprise, since according to the New Age beliefs, God is the "undifferentiated consciousness present in all things," and "all conceptions of God are simply personal expressions of the unknowable truth that mystics encounter." [26] These are some disconcerting realities, which can cause the church to further disconnect and in discouragement to stay at society's margins.

Image-bearing is left to the church, not to the shaman, and it is up to us to thoughtfully bring the reality of God to our unchurched neighbors. In this marketplace engagement, we cannot be perceived as aggressive and abrasive, but as the carriers of the mysterious and the miraculous of the God of the Bible.

Consequences of Postmodernism

In a postmodern, pluralistic society, the all-time challenge remains, to declare transcendent truth in the public arena. Truth cannot be separated from the Word of God. Yet, a Gallup poll shows only about one-third of the American adult population believes the Bible is the actual Word of God and is to be taken literally word for word, relying on its trustworthiness. The rest either feel the Bible is the inspired Word of God, but not literally so, or it is a book of ancient fables, legends, and history as recorded by man. [27] According to the Barna Group:

> A slight majority of Christians (55%) strongly agree the Bible is accurate in all of the principles it teaches, with another 18% agreeing somewhat. About one out of five either disagree strongly (9%) or somewhat (13%) with this statement, and 5% aren't sure what to believe. When faced with the statement that "the Bible, the Koran and the Book of Mormon are all different expressions of the same spiritual truths," the group was evenly split between those who accepted the idea (19% agreed strongly, 22% agreed somewhat) and those who rejected it (28%

disagreed strongly, 12% disagreed somewhat), while leaving a sizeable portion (20%) undecided. [28]

Almost half of the American Christians do not hold a high view of Scripture, and only one-quarter of them have clarity on how the Bible compares to other holy books. Another related survey caused the Barna Group to caution:

> The virtual disappearance of this cornerstone of the Christian faith—that is, God has communicated a series of moral principles in the Bible that are meant to be the basis of our thoughts and actions, regardless of our preferences, feelings or situations—is probably the best indicator of the waning strength of the Christian Church in America today. [29]

The ability to believe simultaneously contradictory things hallmarks the postmodern thinking. Unfortunately, this worldview has infiltrated even the mindset of the American Church. As the postmodern worldview infiltrates how people interpret Scripture, Christians can now make great claims to being the followers of the Word of God, while undermining its very authority. This is why the church should urgently consider the state of faith in our culture and recalibrate for new work, namely re-engaging the public square in order to re-energize the core belief systems of our nation. To do that the church must close the Sunday-to-Monday gap, or the postmodern and the Christian culture will soon look at a chasm between them that will be very hard to cross.

A Real-Life Story—Navigating the Postmodern Families and Their Economics

Victory Church in Yorktown, VA had two things in common with many churches around the country. They had debt and they had a daycare. Co-Pastors Jamé and Jennifer Bolds share how their church has taken this challenge and turned it into an economic blessing for the church and the community's young families. Here is the story in Jamé Bolds own words shared with me in a written interview.

"Zelda walked into my office, sat in my chair and said, "'We are out of room in the preschool. I want a second site.'"

"'What?'" I responded.

"'Our building is at max and we should start a second site. We have a great brand, beautiful staff, and are priced to go the distance.'" Zelda quipped.

"'All right. Let's scale, capitalize, and leverage our assets. Go find us a second building Zelda,'" I said as I started to salsa dance. (At Victory Church we have a culture of excellence and play).

"Most people do not think about the intersection of church life and economics, and it's a shame. People come to church for a large part to get their needs met. They come because they have a problem and they need a solution. Often times those needs are economic. Unfortunately, economics is an issue that pastors often find elusive, fearful, or simply just lack.

"A few simple economic principles rightly understood can transform any church into a ministry that can impact a local economy and develop whole life discipleship.

"When my wife and I came to co-pastor Victory's revitalization, the picture was grim. We were elected with 28 people, the church was in debt $1.3M, the building was in disrepair, we were running a structural deficit of $100,000 a year, the preschool was broke, and the church was living on borrowed time. But God had a plan. Today the balance sheet is completely flipped, and God is doing some powerful work at Victory.

"The turning point was when we began to focus on pastoring the city that God had placed us in. Here's what I mean. We began to ask the question, "What is the spiritual and economic value our church can provide to our city? Often, we pray and ask God to send something or someone, and most of the time the answer we seek is right in front of us. In front of us was a dingy old preschool. We took what was in our hand and sought to make it better. Our deacon board was incredible. (They thought I had lost my mind, but they trusted me.) And we began to rebuild our preschool.

"After weeks of running financial math formulas, we finally discovered a fixed cost structure and an internal rate of return that zeroed out the net present value of money. Gold. (In English, that means we found a way to make money.)

"So, we looked at the preschool that was on life support, took a loan out for $200,000 plus, and rebuilt a commercial-grade style preschool right in the middle of the church. Currently, the preschool is booming, profitable, and debt free. I am excited that we have been able to create value in two major ways: jobs and care.

"We have created eighteen jobs and several management positions that command a serious salary. We have the privilege to employ young married mothers that are re-entering the workforce, single mothers who have struggled, and college students who are working through their degree, and recent high school grads looking for a career. At Victory, we take calling so seriously that if you are with us for ninety days, we will cover 100 percent of the cost of your Child Development Associates credential. We also have the privilege to provide affordable childcare to our twenty to thirty something families. I know nothing about the preschool industry. I just know it is stupid expensive.

"The average costs to a Virginia family for daycare is around $1,600 per month for one child. Let that sink in. That's a mortgage payment, and some young families are making tremendous decisions based on childcare. I have heard stories from our families deciding for one parent to simply stay home or to not have a second or third child because of the childcare costs, or horrifically, I recently heard of a family talking about a second mortgage to pay up front for two years of care.

"For our families and seventy children, we have solved that problem. We provide excellent childcare for under half the cost.

"We were able to move our margin of internal rate of return (IRR) to single digits, thus passing on tremendous savings to our parents. Our economic thinking of lowering our IRR creates the opportunity for young parents to have Christmas, or live in a bigger house. One story that brought tears to my eyes was a professional thirty-something couple decided to have a third child based on the reputation and cost of our preschool.

"A family that enrolled in our preschool started coming to our church and expressed how much we love them because we are thinking of their family's economic life. I have since been able to dedicate their baby and was one of the first to know they were expecting a second. And yes, they already reserved a space in the nursery.

"That's whole-life discipleship at its best—caring and providing for people's faith, work, and economics."

This real-life story of a church for Monday that helps young families flourish economically by providing affordable childcare can inspire other churches to find assets can build income flow for the church and bless their communities. Asking questions at the intersection of church life and economics, and bringing answers based on compassion and appropriate capacity helps both the sustainability of the church and the financial stability of its families, thus leading to spiritual and economic thriving.

What Are the Spiritual Currents in Western Culture?

Pining for a Clean Slate

I sometimes sigh, "It was easier to evangelize in Bulgaria than in the States." In reality, it is difficult to evangelize in both settings, but for different reasons. Bulgaria, part of the Eastern bloc countries at the time I was growing up, had forgotten its roots in Christianity. The nation's faith, once an Eastern Orthodox country, was tested as an aggressive oppressor came on the scene in 1944—the communist regime that argued there is no God. By the time the 80's rolled around, two generations had been taught godlessness and evolution at school, and there was barely any memory left of the Christian tenets that once shaped Bulgaria's belief system.

What I experienced, as a young person with zeal to evangelize, was a common occurrence. If Christians could find open-minded people willing to consider a higher power, those conversations often resulted in conversions. People's slates were clean. They held to no other theology to fight the Christian one, and some even questioned the legitimacy of the communist, atheistic ideology. The Christian faith in Bulgaria, under communist persecution, saw the darkest of times and the brightest of times. Amidst cultural and government persecution, the Spirit-filled church was flourishing, its buildings were bursting at the seams with attendance numbers exceeding their seating capacity, and many believers were evangelizing, risking the life they had in order to see others have what they found in Jesus.

Fast-forward to today's postmodern, post-Christian, North American experience. It is difficult to evangelize people who think they are Christian enough. All paths lead to God, and they believe their good works will get them to heaven. The Barna Group says, "Christians must realize we are not doing evangelism on a clean slate. Cultural perceptions and Christianity's poor reputation are actively de-converting people raised in church and hardening non-Christians against evangelistic efforts." [1]

It is a good thing to be a culturally Christian nation until it is not. People judge the Christian faith by the Christian messengers. This should have been a good thing, but has turned out to be a bad thing. As the popular entertainment show, The Weakest Link, taught us, we are only as strong as our weakest link. In the West, we attempt to build Christian cultures on the shoulders of cultural Christians— the weakest link. Yet, most people, although not practicing Christians, still call themselves Christians, and it is hard for the unchurched to know who's who, so they reject it all because they watch us all.

Many things were questionable under communism, but one thing was clear—who's who. Christianity in Bulgaria was not worn as identity politics, a symbol of pride, or designation for economic freedom. Under persecution, no one is Christian in name only. Who would want to bear the badge of Christ if they were not willing to bear the image of Christ? That was too high of a price to pay. That is why, when people were bold enough to listen to the Christian message, they usually were bold enough to accept it, because they had been watching the messengers and believed what they saw.

Christians in Bulgaria often lost their reputations, friends, jobs, ivy league-school-admissions, and career and sport advancements. Because of our Christian faith, my own family was persecuted. My father was denied college admission, my grandfather-in-law was imprisoned, and I was harassed and questioned by the police. Being Christians in a culture that despised Christianity cost us financial and social capital, but we chose to do it anyway.

The persecution produced the opposite result the communist ruling party desired. Instead of giving up on faith in God, the external pressure clarified and fortified the internal beliefs in people and formed them into committed followers of Jesus. The question is, "How, without external pressure, will believers in America remain or become faithful and fruitful?"

Admittedly, there is a different dynamic when one lives in a free, wealthy, materialistic, hedonistic, self-centered, entertainment-saturated, powerful society. People's attention is divided, usually focused on self-improvement and self-fulfillment. Their loyalty hops from one cause to another, and they can find many ways to satisfy their wants. The deep cry of a soul without God is not experienced as deeply as in less developed communities around the world, because often people anesthetize their pain with their pursuit of pleasure. Thus, need-based evangelism is not as powerful. That is why building a Sunday-to-Monday Connect Bridge to the unchurched that we talked about in Chapter 3 is so important. Integrating our faith into the marketplace through on-ramps for both committed Christians and sceptics, agnostics, and nones to interact while participating in the economy gives real opportunities for relationship-building and value sharing as we get to know each other.

The Church for Monday models practical ways of translating the gospel to a hedonistic culture. As we saw, the more developed the community, the less "felt" need of God that community has. One good way to reach economically developed cultures is through their economies. It is imperative in those settings we practice consistent, holistic faith right where we are—work, home, school, or play. We can discover points of connections with the unchurched and build integration on-ramps in order to share our convictions in a culturally legible way and incline unbelievers toward faith.

This approach to evangelism is not programmatic and fast. It is much more involved and many times slower than quoting scripture verses to passersby's at an outreach campaign. Patience and commitment are two values desperately needed in North American evangelism today, yet often lacking in our "microwave" culture of fast results. Successful evangelism is not about the ease with which we can lead someone to profess Christ, but about discipling people to genuinely live out their Christian faith both in persecuted and in free societies. America is one of the easiest places in which to become a Christian, but one of the hardest places to genuinely live the Christian life.

Friends, it is time for the faithful church to evangelize anew to our Postmodern, Post-Christian; Post-truth society by giving of ourselves what costs us the most—time, selfish ambition, entertainment, money, leisure—you can finish the list that costs you the most. We cannot enter the marketplace to innovate, love, and live on mission without counting the cost to walk with Jesus where He walks. If we miscount, it will cost Jesus what it did not cost us—souls heading to eternal separation instead of eternal salvation. It is obvious the clean slate is not the tablet we write on when image-bearing the gospel in America. Yet, giving ourselves to evangelism is finding convincing ways in the public arena to be the open epistles God is forming us to become, so the unchurched can say: "We have been watching you, and we believe what we have seen."

New Challenges for Christians

The signs of change permeate every sphere of the twenty-first-century society—social, cultural, political, economic, and religious. The world has made a transition to a new historical paradigm, the postmodernism, which is "a new way of viewing reality."[2] This new worldview represents a reaction against the confidence of the post-Enlightenment modernist period. It rejects the authority of reason and science, and it rebels against rigid boundaries and structures. The heart of postmodernism is denial of the reality of a unified world as the object of human perception. The postmodern era has replaced knowledge with interpretation.[3] Truth is seen as relative, not absolute, and one's opinion and feelings, thus, take center stage to the point of being new absolutes—but always in conflict with those of others.

Robert Webber cites "A Call to an Ancient Evangelical Future" as he sounds a wake-up call on what this means for the Christian faith:

> At one time the Western world was narrated by the Christian God and the biblical story of his work in Israel and through Jesus to redeem and restore the whole creation. Today, this story of God's cosmic salvation has

been lost in the West. In Europe the light has nearly flickered out, and in North America the light is growing dim. New challenges now appear on the horizon. [4]

Reductionism of the Gospel

Darrell Guder, a scholar in evangelism and church growth, identifies the internal challenges the church faces as gospel reductionism. He asserts the Western reductionism "attempts to reduce the gospel, to bring it under control, to render it intellectually respectable, or to make it serve another agenda than God's purposes."[5] Webber also critiques the reductionism, identifying secularism as the basic culprit: "Secularism has won on three accounts: (1) by challenging the cosmic dimension of the gospel, (2) by forcing Christians to reduce the gospel to our personal journey, and (3) by inducing Christians to defend the gospel by means of reason and science."[6]

Webber urges Christians to study their contemporary situation and the historical developments that got them there so they can employ the biblical-theological narrative to influence society's formation.[7] The ancient church understood the cosmic narrative of God's story and led in the arts, in learning, and in the sciences,[8] but the contemporary church no longer shapes its world according to the biblical premises of God's involvement in the world through creation, incarnation, and re-creation.

Secularization: Sacred/Secular Divide

Christian faith is uniquely qualified to narrate the world and to give shape to all world cultures and civilizations. To accomplish that divine mandate, Christians need to fully grasp the biblical understanding of redemption: God redeemed *all of life* by the cross and the empty tomb, not just the human soul. The assumption the soul is the only true essence of the person and needs to be redeemed from the sinfulness of the body comes from Gnostic origins. If Christ came only to save souls, then the rest of the world is unredeemable.

The historical split of sacred and secular became the tipping point for the secularization of the West: "This split occurred because the understanding of the incarnation was reduced from God who *became* the created order to God who *stepped* into the creation," from God who took all the effects of fallen humanity spread throughout his creation to a god who stepped into history to save souls without a broader cosmic agenda.[10] Amy Sherman, a contemporary voice for the integration of faith and work, laments this reductionism: "Jesus' work is not exclusively about our individual salvation, but about the cosmic redemption and renewal of all things. It is not just about our reconciliation to a holy God, though that is the beautiful center of it. It is also about our reconciliation with one another and with the creation itself."[11] She agrees with Dallas Willard's similar contentions concerning the anemic privatized gospel that has permeated the message of contemporary Christianity.[12] We cannot allow the schism between sacred and secular to continue, otherwise, the reductionism of the gospel will perpetuate the powerless state of the church.

Syncretism: Thirst for the "Spiritual"

Even though secularism undermines the Christian narrative, people still hunger for enchantment. Cheryl Bridges Johns says the fastest growing group in the U.S. is not a denomination, but a group of spiritual, yet non-Christian religious people.[13] The lens through which these people perceive ultimate reality and the purpose of life has been influenced by a range of religions, philosophies, ideologies, and spiritualities—"from astrology to Zen, from capitalism to Marxism, from new age to Scientology, from ESP to UFOs, and so on."[14] This secularized but religious context presents a formidable challenge for Western church leaders.[15]

This emerging syncretism is the new religious synthesis. James Herrick estimates that one to two thousand new religious movements have arisen in the United States alone in the twentieth century, with only a few of them holding to traditional Judeo-Christian theology.[16]

One can feel the impact of the change everywhere—in the marketplace and in politics, at work and at school; at the end, it is widely popularized through the media. Spirituality is no longer confined to the sanctuary and synagogue. Herrick observes pervasive alternative spiritualities have moved into "the lecture hall and the classroom, the movie theater and the surgical theater, the corporate office and the Oval Office." [17] The new Western spirituality is an eclectic mix of religious and spiritual ideas, beliefs, and practices, which persist despite the lack of institutionalization, simply relying on loosely bound networks of practitioners, the publishing industry, and the media. For that reason, we see expanding "beliefs in angels and reincarnation, greater appeal of religious and quasi-religious shrines, retreat centers, and theme parks, interest in metaphysical, theosophical teachings; and 'possibility thinking'; and large proportions of Americans reporting mystical experiences." [18]

Without a doubt, this new spiritual landscape with its desire for the mysterious, the spiritual, and the religious, but not Christian, is a challenge to the church in America. What stumps us could also help us if we are willing to adjust. There is an open door for evangelism because there is openness to pretty much everything. Yet, unless we re-tool our evangelistic toolbox, we will miss this opportunity.

Finding what people's pain points are will give us the opportunity to bring God's healing to their "wounds." There is a plethora of pain points in our economically-developed America, but we need to discover them and not assume we know them. Smart businesses do social listening before they do marketing of their solutions. We have something of greater value than any business does. The Holy Spirit has prepared a receptive place for God's solution in the hearts of people. Let's listen to uncover where it is; then model the solution, do not just tell.

Evangelism is:

- Listen

- Walk

- Talk

Yet, sometimes we do gospel-sharing in reverse. We strike a conversation, not to listen but to tell. Then, we halfway hear and quickly move on as though we have a quota to fill before we walk the talk. We need to ask ourselves, "How is that working for the church?" If it is not, and I suggest it isn't, then we need to revise how we share our faith in a post-Christian society.

Individualism: An Individualized Gospel

Since the beginning of modern Western consciousness, which arose with the ideas of Descartes, Christianity has become increasingly individualized. The new arena of alternative spirituality became available with the cultural shift to the postmodern worldview now permeating even some Christian communities. Guder sees it as part of a larger historical context:

> As a result of the historical process of the separation of church and state, and the progressive disestablishment of religion, the Christian presence has also been privatized. Faith communities are looked upon as inappropriate themes for public discourse. Public culture is in the main agnostic, and the primary emphasis when religion does come up is upon the need for tolerance. [19]

Guder emphatically denounces the dichotomy that results from an individualized approach to the gospel. It has reduced the gospel message to the fundamental evangelistic question: "Are you saved?" Christians have capitalized on the benefits of salvation to the neglect of the reason for which they have received God's grace, to empower them in becoming Christ's witnesses. He insists, "This fundamental choice between the benefits of the gospel and the mission of the gospel constitutes the most profound reductionism of the gospel." [20] Consequently, the church has become unsure of itself and incapable of persuasive witness, because it has not formulated a gospel that can break through the individualization and privatization of religion.

The current society desperately needs to hear the proclamation of God's missional gospel in all spheres of life. Christopher Wright defines God's mission this way: "Fundamentally, our mission (if it is biblically informed and validated) means our committed participation as God's people, at God's invitation and command, in God's own mission within the history of God's world for the redemption of God's creation."[21] When the church once again reinvigorates its understanding of God's mission and His gospel's holistic agenda, the result will be a re-envisioned purpose, and hopefully an invigorated re-entry in the public arena. Will the public arena accept this in any way? That is a fair question to ask and an answer not ours to give. For we cannot make the marketplace accept our witness, but we can clothe our witness with compassion and the capacity to make a real-life difference in our communities. We do not profess an exclusively private gospel, but one that strengths cities, states, and countries. That is why an emergence of churches who understand the significance of God's redemption purposes for our Mondays, not just for our Sundays, is essential for the holistic reach of the gospel, and for the closing of the Sunday-to-Monday reductionism gap.

A Real -Life Story— Incarnating the Gospel in its Community's Darkest Places

Alfred D. Hughes' Unit is a prison for men in the Texas Department of Criminal Justice located in Gatesville, Texas. Executive Pastor, John Cruz, of Northplace Church in Sacse, Texas, has reimagined what prison ministry looks like and is transforming the lives of offenders and prison guards alike–from the inside out. Here is Northplace's story shared with me by Cruz in a written interview.

Inside the stone walls of Alfred D. Hughes Unit penitentiary, Pastor Cruz and his team planted a campus of Northplace Church, a multi-site church led by Pastor Bryan Jarrett in North Dallas. In the past this penitentiary rated as one of the highest in Texas for sexual assaults; in addition, 55 percent of the prisoners are over forty years old. Offenders struggle with mental illness, physical aggression, overcrowding, gang violence, racism, and drugs. Statistics show that within three years of being released, many prisoners are placed back into the system. Many of the prisoners are broken and in desperate need of emotional healing from within.

Bound by their physical barriers, going to church is impossible, so Northplace brought the church to the offenders. Cruz says, "We saw an opportunity to not only share the gospel, but to show the gospel by pouring into a different demographic of people to teach them more about God and how to apply biblical principles to life inside and outside the barb-wire fences." Northplace partners with prison guards and other faith ministries integrating methods, services, and the expertise of existing staff and volunteers. These partnerships broaden the reach in supporting not only the prison offenders, but also the prison guards in building their faith within everyday work.

Northplace Church planted a branch of their home church, right in jail where the darkness is the densest, because their goal is to give offenders an opportunity to receive faith, to become part of a supportive church community and contribute to society once re-entered back into the community. Offenders attend career workshops, college admission programs, and serve in the church in training to gain leadership, management, and spiritual disciplines in order to transform their lives from the inside out. The church helps offenders restore their human dignity so they can live lives that honor God and others. "Biblical community," Cruz says, "is vital for an individual to continue to grow in faith. Discipleship and leadership development happen ineffectively in isolation; therefore, we commit to foster true spiritual growth by creating a culture of community through *Northplace Groups*.

As the community grows, Cruz and his team are looking to initiatives where prisoners serve others in the community, do mission work remotely, and show genuine love to the people around them. Cruz says, "The character of Christ is never more clearly displayed than when individuals and the church embrace the pain and poverty of others with grace and compassion. At Northplace, we express this compassion by serving our neighbors locally and abroad wherever the trail of pain takes us.

This story teaches us much by way of modeling what a Church for Monday can do even in one of the most broken areas of our marketplace. The church's team is awakening the spiritual desire within offenders and developing a true community of believers among the prison church. While Northplace Church continues to establish itself inside of the barbed wire fences, their goal is to teach missions, influence cultural and personal renewal, and redefine the role of the church in prison ministry.

On Mission with God in a Twenty-First Century World

A Surprising Place for Mission

My first image about the United States was inspired by my college professor who taught the class of modern architecture while I was studying for my Master's degree in landscape architecture. She had just returned from the "land of plenty" and was deeply impressed by her American experience. In order to illustrate what the most developed country in the world and its modern architecture looked like, she began to describe what she had seen at the Mall of America in Minneapolis. She told us of shopping in enormous, covered spaces that had street-like paths without cars, all-glass elevators, gardens, and even roller coasters. And food, food, food everywhere! Not only was food plentiful in the United States, but it was also enormous, especially the hot dogs. As much as the architecture of the Mall of America had impressed my professor, the hot dog vendors didn't have a rival in the world, because their hot dogs were an entire foot-long and so were their buns.

To this impressionable twenty-one-year-old college student, my professor's stories sounded like fairy tales. I vividly remember thinking I would likely never get to see the foot-long hot dogs and would ride in all-glass elevators only in my dreams because of where I was born. However, God had a different plan for my life. He made a way for me to not only come to America, but to become an American citizen. In our great desire for freedom, political and religious, and dreams of becoming an entrepreneur, my family took a leap of faith. My husband and I and our nine-month-old baby girl, immigrated to the land of plenty and the land of faith when the Berlin wall fell. It has been more than twenty years since becoming a naturalized citizen and now I do my part in building the American dream. I often forget to look at our American life through the fresh eyes I brought when I arrived, but one thing I vividly remember is how surprised I was to discover my expectations of finding vibrant faith (in a country which does its commerce with a currency inscription "In God We Trust") fell short of the reality.

While my family came from a land of scarcity, we belonged to the persecuted church in Bulgaria, which had rich, powerful, and resilient faith. I was part of a church that was ready at any given time to risk everything for our faith in Jesus Christ. You might be wondering if the Christians in Bulgaria needed us more than the believers in the States. I believe, in God's providence, He brought us here precisely because we knew material impoverishment, but lived in spiritual riches so we may encourage our American brothers and sisters.

As a place of historical revivals, the American church has sent hundreds of thousands of missionaries abroad, but now it is time to look into our own backyard and evangelize anew the 76 percent of Americans who do not wake up on Sunday morning looking to go to church. [1] If a separate nation, the number of unchurched people in America would make the eighth most populous country in the world. [2] Sometimes it feels as though I have undertaken a reverse missionary journey to reignite radical faith for God's radical mission in the very seedbed of missionary senders.

Yet the church in America continues to see the mission field abroad as its primary missionary responsibility. The Great Commission Jesus left his followers has a well-defined stewardship map. Acts 1:8 has it starting with our own Jerusalem—the community in which we live, work, and go to school. Mission starts in the community we know best, because it gives us the opportunity to love best. For if we don't love the neighbor we see, how can we say we love the God whom we do not see (1 John 4:20)?

Because America has become a mission field, the American Church is faced with the necessity to entrepreneurially re-envision its mission in order to regain ground for the Kingdom? As we've already discussed, the future of the church is in high-touch, experience-based environments offering deep value and meaning. For that reason, we need to build relationships with the unchurched if we want to flourish our communities. Questions such as: "Where is our place of mission?" and "How can we re-tool the way we do mission at home?" can be the catalyst not only for transforming the unchurched but the churched as well. What if we start sending more missionaries into our own backyard than abroad? Admittedly, we send missionaries at home, but not at the same rate or with the same excitement and financial support as we send them abroad. While doing that, what if church leaders start teaching believers to live as a missional community, practicing *corporate witness* in all spheres of society? Churches which equip their congregations for Monday and embed themselves in the local economy give us a practical example of how we can do that in our own communities. If we embrace the Church for Monday model, we just might lay the foundation for a new awakening about God and faith in the West.

It's worth noting, Jesus entrusted the Great Commission not to single individuals, but to a missional community of followers–His disciples turned apostles, who were to carry on a corporate witness. A fresh look at the church's witness not only as scattered believers, but also as a gathered body, undoubtedly will re-establish our biblical foundation of being the people of God with a Great Commission to fulfill and a Great Commandment to practice.

Compelling Reasons for Mission

Most of us know in our gut things have changed when it comes to faith in America. Colson and Pearcey label the dominant culture today as both post-Christian and postmodern. They describe the post-Christians as "Americans, along with most other Western cultures, who no longer rely on Judeo-Christian truths as the basis of their public philosophy or their moral consensus. [3] As a result, the church in America has lost its privileged position as a moral herald. Our neighbors do not run first to the church for guidance on relationship building, marriage, childbearing, child rearing, elderly care, or prison reform. As a matter of fact, it is just the opposite. When issues arise in our communities, it seems the last place people are looking for answers, is in the church. Separation between the secular and the sacred spheres of life has become so commonplace in America that even many Christians struggle to find ways to integrate their faith with their daily lives. I have often observed believers intellectually assent to integrating work and faith or God and business, yet, in practice, they keep separate compartments for the secular and the sacred.

Twenty-first-century cultural shifts affect the whole of society and have not spared the church. The Christian church now increasingly occupies a place in the margins of society. In fact, it is fair to say the church in America is undergoing a crisis. The number of people willing to associate with a church has declined significantly. The Barna Group's tracking of data since 1996 shows an alarming trend: a sharp rise in those identifying as atheists, agnostic, or "none"/no faith, alongside a nearly matching decline in "born again" Christians. [4]

These changes have brought the church to a crucial juncture. All the church has been needs re-evaluation. All the church will become must consider the stamp of the current times, or the church will find itself even further on the fringe of society's attention. To most local churches, the notion the church has a place in the marketplace and its economy, for the benefit of both the churched and the unchurched, remains a foreign concept.

Many Christians prefer a separate church and state existence, in which the *do's* and *don'ts* are clearly stated, but life in the Kingdom is not just a matter of avoiding what is wrong. Believers cannot effectively serve as Jesus' apprentices unless they integrate their jobs and everyday activities into the Kingdom. Many support this detachment from secular society by adopting a fatalistic understanding of an apocalyptic line of thought. [5] Although God works behind the scenes and beyond human history, we need to remember He still works in partnership with humans.

The danger is, if Christians focus exclusively on the future world, they may reduce existence in the *now* to a mere end-time waiting room. Such a mindset further alienates the church from the real world, causing it to lose even more ground in Western culture. As this continues, attendance will continue to plunge, and our neighbors will frequent our churches less and less because we are abandoning the public arena.

If you are reading this book you likely agree with me that a dichotomized existence only paints us into a corner and prevents us from exploring new ways to frame the gospel for cultural application so our post-Christian communities can hear it. As pastors we have the privilege, but also the challenging task to equip people for works of service (Eph. 4:12), which extend beyond the church walls. This is easier said than done. Most of us have tried and often didn't succeed. Our culture accosts believers with wealth, materialism, entertainment, messages of self-fulfillment, sex, and power—all things which distract believers from living out the mission of God. Still, we can teach holistic spirituality and integrated faith, but we have to employ new methods for different results.

For example, to believers with wealth and focused on personal gains, the pastor can offer a richer biblical understanding of stewardship by pointing to a prayerful consideration of the kinds of investments they can make to start, or scale up, an existing business to advance the community and their own family. Every time an entrepreneur solves an important problem, and makes the living conditions better, his or her community flourishes. When we do creative work, we display the image of our Creator. Churches that prepare their congregations for influence on Monday offer to their people practical guidance in how to make a difference in the marketplace. If we teach our congregations we can approach work as worship, the opening of a small business as a missional endeavor, and the leading of a corporation as ushering Kingdom principles in dark places, we will be preparing the local church for integrated faith.

I believe we can regain public credibility if we faithfully reenter the marketplace to flourish our neighborhoods. Although I understand we are facing an upward battle to engage a very busy, often dismissing culture, especially when dealing with rising issues of anxiety, drug addictions, crime, infertility, and broken family relationships. Yet, we cannot hide from the difficult realities of our communities; neither can we wait to address them only if they walk through our church doors. If we desire to live missionally, then we cannot live separately. It is time for the body of Christ to get out of its Sunday real estate bubble and strategically engage the Monday marketplace. The New Testament is clear God's Spirit forms a community for mission. "God's call has always formed a people, a community, within which God was known, worshiped, made known, and served." [6] The work of the church to make God known to an unchurched world is more needed than ever, although it seems more challenging than ever.

Tom Nelson, President of Made to Flourish and pastor of a local, multi-site church, says that "Holy Scripture speaks a good deal about economic flourishing. Yet, in our personal lives, in our congregations, and in our work, we all too often woefully neglect to connect the gospel of the Kingdom with economics. This harms our witness, our cities, and our future. The church needs to address and begin the hard work of overcoming the perilous Sunday-to-Monday gap." [7]

In recent years, God has stirred His church to recognize He is a God of all life and that a sharp divide between the sacred and secular does not fit His agenda. Unless believers understand and practice an integrated expression of work-ministry-worship-family, the local church will become an irrelevant community.

God Is Leading His Church on Mission

The uncreated God is a triune, loving community and wants people to realize their full created potential in fellowship with Himself. [8] Yet, humans revolted against God and His rightful authority as the creator and preserver of life. Consequently, all people succumb to sin's bondage and became a part of Satan's kingdom of darkness. Although people cannot redeem this situation, God can reverse their darkened state.

Abraham Kuyper, twentieth-century theologian and prime minister of the Netherlands, saw sin's darkening in this, that people lost the gift of grasping the true context, the proper coherence, and the systematic integration of all things: "Now we view everything only externally, not in its core and essence, each thing individually, but not in their mutual connection and in their origin from God." [9] No wonder we segregate life in compartments and have a hard time integrating our faith in business, government, education, arts and entertainment, media and technology. Especially, in the light that humanity forfeited God's creation design and altered the relationship between Creator and creation. People's relationships with God and with one another are forever affected. We cannot remedy any of that on our own.

Yet, God retains full control and leads His people on mission. In His love for all humanity, He commissions instruments of mission. He started with Abraham and the nation of Israel, then sent His Son, then the Holy Spirit, and finally the church. The nature of the Trinity is missionary. "Mission is the heartbeat of God. Father, Son, and Holy Spirit are all involved in the missionary endeavor: the Father's love compels missions, the Son's ministry exemplifies missions, and the Spirit's power and illumination guide missionary activity." [10]

The Abrahamic Covenant ensured God's blessings to all who are children of Abraham through faith. God desires all people enjoy the blessing of abundance, innovation, fruitfulness, creativity, long life, peace, and rest within the context of healthy relationships with Himself and with others. We read in Genesis 12 that God committed Himself to bless Abraham and to bring blessing to all nations through Abraham's seed:

> The LORD had said to Abram,
>
> "Go from your country, your people and your father's household to the land I will show you.
>
> I will make you into a great nation,
>
> and I will bless you;
>
> I will make your name great,
>
> and you will be a blessing.
>
> I will bless those who bless you,
>
> and whoever curses you I will curse;
>
> and all peoples on earth
>
> will be blessed through you.'"

That promise required Abraham's faith and obedience, then his offspring's commitment to the ethical demands of the covenant (18:19). The Abrahamic covenant is a moral agenda for God's people as well as a mission statement by God. [11] The New Testament's Great Commission can be understood fully only in light of the Old Testament's history of mission: "The mission that God takes on Himself in His categorical commitments to Abraham and His offspring, and the mission that God lays on Abraham in consequence—'Be a blessing.'" [12]

The relationships between Creator and creation had been radically fractured (Gen. 3–11), but the Abrahamic Covenant provided a hope-filled framework for the *missio Dei*—the mission of God in human history, which culminated in the redemptive work of Jesus Christ (Gal. 3:16). Our faith is anchored on the fact that in Christ alone, through the gospel of His death and resurrection, stands the hope of blessing for all nations. [13]

As the people of God, the twenty-first-century church carries the same responsibility for the demands placed on Abraham's posterity (Gen. 18:19). Through the Spirit's wooing (Eph. 2:2) and the church's compelling testimony (Acts 1:8), the *missio Dei* extends anywhere depravity and rejection of the gospel prevail. Although the promise in Genesis 12 came to its fulfillment in Christ, the church still bears an indispensable role for the continued realization of *missio Dei*. It is worth noting that the Abrahamic Covenant offered blessing to non-Israelites. In like manner, the church has to seek intentionally those who are outside of the family of faith in order to fulfill God's divine intent.

Compelled by the love of Christ, we partner with God in His reconciliation work in the world (2 Cor. 5:14–21). "It is not so much the case that God has a mission for His church in the world, as that God has a church for His mission in the world. Mission was not made for the church; the church was made for mission—God's mission." [14] The *missio Dei* is all-creation encompassing and reaching all spheres of life. It focuses on the church's development into the reality of God's new creation, in order to become a credible witness to God and a blessing to the nations. God does not have a plan B. The church is God's first and only plan A for reaching the lost. It is especially important to have the church's witness in the marketplace, where the majority of the harvest can be found since the majority of people spend the majority of their waking hours at their place of work and business.

Sent to Reconcile

God the Father sent[15] Jesus the Son on a reconciliation mission (2 Cor. 5:18a, 21). This mission did not just suddenly appear in the New Testament. Matthew introduces Jesus as "the son of David, the son of Abraham" (Matt. 1:1). This introduction pulls the cohesive thread of God's mission throughout Old and New Testaments. By combining the Abrahamic and Davidic covenants, Matthew highlights the universal significance of the One who would, as son of Abraham, fulfill what was promised for Abraham's seed (blessing for all nations), and as son of David, would exercise the prophesied messianic reign over all the earth. [16] It is important for us to see that Matthew begins his Gospel with Jesus the Messiah as the son of Abraham and ends it with the mission mandate that would encompass all nations. The New Testament church inherits the authority of the Abrahamic mission and in this way is sent to be an instrument of blessing anywhere in the world.

To fulfill the Abrahamic promise, God the Father offered the Son as atonement on behalf of fallen humanity (Rom. 3:25–26). Whoever believes in Him (John 3:16) will be richly blessed (Rom. 10:12), will be saved (Rom: 10:13), and have eternal life (John 3:16). Scripture states, "the Son of Man came to seek and to save what was lost" [17] (ἀπόλλυμι, [18] Luke 19:10). Jesus came to restore everything that had been ἀπόλλυμi (*apollimi*). The word *apollimi* means destroyed to the point of no return. The purpose of the Abrahamic promise, "be a blessing," is missional, and it is not bound in time or geography, because it focuses on restoring everything humans have fractured and all that has been destroyed to the point of no return.

This state of brokenness (*apollimi*), permeates everything humans touch at home, work, and play. There is no place and no person that has been spared the devastation of separation from God. Depraved humans don't know what they are missing. One cannot know what one has not experienced. That is why Jesus sends His church to make Him known, and the Holy Spirit empowers the church to become a foretaste of King Jesus and His righteous domain. No human efforts could ever recover the intimacy between Creator and creation, only Jesus could reconcile "all things" to God (Col. 1:20). Humankind had lost entrance to the throne of God, but

Jesus restored its standing with God the Father (Eph. 3:12), and now the Spirit bears witness of adoption in all believers (Rom. 8:15) and empowers them to witness (Acts 1:8).

People truly flourish only when they enjoy a relationship with God. Unbelievers commonly sense a void within themselves and desire more of life, regardless of their apparent success. In Jesus Christ, God offers fallen humanity a way back to Himself, and in the church, He presents the world with the message of reconciliation.

At the consummation of times, all people will recognize and worship the one true God. The church is the one that bears witness to the only true God. For that reason, the role of the church as a transformation agent in God's purpose, for the life of the world, is irreplaceable. That is why this question begs an answer: What does it mean for the church to be biblically faithful, theologically informed, and missionally aligned to be God's redemptive tool in the twenty-first century postmodern, post-Christian world? The contemporary church must wrestle honestly and discern prayerfully how to live with a robust faith in the marketplace.

A Real-Life Story—Practicing God's Mission in a Twenty-first Century World

Mosaic is an entrepreneurial church known to make positive disruption through innovative ideas and techniques. It intentionally integrates itself in the marketplace and re-connects with lapsed and non-Christians from diverse ethnic backgrounds. Here is Mosaic's story shared with me by Pastor Mark DeYmaz and as described in his book *Disruption*.

> In the University District of Little Rock, Arkansas, Mark and Linda DeYmaz planted Mosaic church in 2002. [19] As its capital city, people traveled through the entire state to visit and to shop there. Things began to change however in the early 90s when gangs became problematic. The city's gang problem centered in and around the University District. A once-vibrant community became a place of high crime, homelessness, and poverty. [20]

Pastor and entrepreneur, Mark DeYmaz, wanted to revitalize this community through disruptive innovation to impact its people for Christ. He says:

The extent of my initial vision was to plant a church in which men and women of varying ethnic diversity could worship God together as one. At the time, I had not considered the spiritual, social, and financial challenges we would face in establishing such a church or the corresponding complexities of multiethnic, missional, and urban congregations. God led us step-by-step through the years until we recognized how to overcome the obstacles through disruptive innovation and ultimately how to repurpose the church to redeem the community." [21] At the beginning, the congregation met in two different church facilities until they found an abandoned Walmart to sublease. Despite having a consistent place, from the start Mosaic was not constricted to four walls. In August 2002, two Hispanic women began attending services. A Hispanic leader saw an opportunity to make a difference in the trailer park they lived in. Many undocumented immigrants lived side by side with economically challenged blacks and whites. Mosaic church purchased a trailer and set about improving it. They went in two-person teams door to door, each team consisting of English and Spanish speakers. "We introduced ourselves," DeYmaz says, "surveyed the community, inviting residents to share with us physical, material, educational, social, and spiritual needs we could meet. We were successful in establishing tutoring services, replacing windows, offering dental services, leading Bible studies, teaching women English, and investing time by building a community. As a result, twenty-six of them became followers of Christ. [22]

The Leadership of Mosaic church stays aware of the needs of the community. In order to flourish their neighbors, DeYmaz launched Village and Vine, their own non-profit that helps other non-profits, projects, organizations, and startup businesses begin with the right materials and resources. Village and Vine is an umbrella non-profit that invests in its community by partnering with organizations who are wishing to do something in the community. They offer incubation, short-term support, central services, tax preparation services, and professional consulting for projects that fall under the mission and vision of the organization. [23]

The mission of Village and Vine is to improve the quality of life for people living in and around the University District by providing just and affordable opportunities to address social, material, and physical needs to redeem the community. [24]

Jon, an elder at Mosaic church says, "I have come to understand that to truly transform a community, a church cannot simply focus on things spiritual. I continue to see the benefits and fruit in the approach of spiritual, social, and financial disruption." [25]

This real-life story of an entrepreneurial church for Monday encourages us to practice holistic spirituality and re-envision the mission of the church, so the church in America can be a place of influence and change. The church's goal should be to meet the spiritual, but also the practical, everyday needs of its city. Just like Mosaic church and Pastor Mark DeYmaz' team, churches across North America can be innovative disruptors as they seek the Holy Spirit's wisdom to address their unique communities' needs in order to experience culture transformation and kingdom advancement.

Outside of the Church Walls

A Harvest That Cries Out

Our post-Christian, postmodern culture, with its moral decadence, philosophical options, and religious pluralism, practically cries out to the church in an inaudible voice to notice the harvest is ready to be brought in. People of the culture typically don't think this way, but the dysfunctional emptiness of their lives is what cries out. As I answered the call to vocational ministry, God showed me a vivid image of the harvest.

In my mind, I saw a compelling picture of desperate people who, on the outside, looked exactly like you and me. They were wearing everyday clothes—no holes, wrinkles, or stains. Their faces were clean, their pace was busy, and they were intently focused on staying on top of life. No one in that crowd stood out of place, evoked pity, or caused attention. They looked like ordinary people except for their extraordinary mouths. Their mouths were gaping black holes. The people I saw were passing by me with mouths wide open in an abysmal, yet inaudible scream. Since, they were crying out only on the inside, no one was paying attention to them. Although they didn't have tears on the outside, they had gaping holes on the inside. Church people were passing them by without giving them a second glance as they looked for worthier subjects of their missional affection.

This picture of the harvest that the Holy Spirit gave me twice, ripped me apart. It stopped me in my tracks and has not let go since. I want to be a Kingdom harvest worker that recognizes when the "wheat" is ready to be gathered for fruitfulness instead of passed by in forgetfulness. God commissions His Spirit-empowered church to bear incarnational witness to His power for an inside-out transformation. If we want to reach our communities for Christ, we must prove the church's reality to a disbelieving world. Only then the world might reconsider its skepticism and hostility.

A Ministry of Reconciliation

To remind ourselves that to take part in the cosmic plan of God we must be refueled anew with joy and meaning. God was pleased to have His fullness dwell in Jesus Christ (Col. 1:19) who became the head of "the body, the Church" (1:18). Jesus, in turn, filled the church with His essence (Eph. 1:23), conferred His glory on it (John 17: 22), equipped it with His Spirit (Acts 2:4) and sent (*apostellō*) it into the world, much as God the Father had sent (*apostellō*) Him into the world (John 17:18).

Robert Scudieri describes elements of that sent-ness, or so-called *shaliach*, in the Jewish tradition that carried over to the Christian apostleship (*apostellō*). First, the apostle is one who is commissioned. A person could not simply choose to become someone else's apostle. Second, the commissioning brought with it the authority to represent the other, to be the other person in another place. All of the authority held by the sender is carried by the one sent. Third, this authorization is for a specific purpose. There is a task to be accomplished and the authority of the apostle is extended only for this task.[1]

The role of the church is significant as Jesus' witness in the world. "The church is where Christ dwells in His fullness (Eph.1:20–23), and where God reveals to creation the unlimited expression of His wisdom as far as the earth is concerned (2:10)."[2] As we discussed, the church is not God's contingency plan. "Rather, it is a mystery, the masterpiece God has been saving until last . . . wherein God displays the grace that breaks down the dividing wall between a Jew and Gentile, and between humanity and Himself."[3]

Because the church continues the incarnational expression of Christ, God has entrusted it with the ministry and message of reconciliation: "All this is from God, who reconciled us to Himself through Christ and gave us the ministry of reconciliation: that God was reconciling the world to Himself in Christ, not counting men's sins against them. And He has committed to us the message of reconciliation" (2 Cor. 5:18–19). The missional community of believers takes up the ministry and message of reconciliation. Believers become the full representation of Christ, as they practice a love-obey relationship with Him (John 15:9–10) and follow His servant-leadership example in their local churches, communities, schools, corporate and business settings, and family and public environments.

Spirit Empowered for Mission and Kingdom Witness

Churches which prepare their congregations for Monday seek the empowerment of the Holy Spirit to pursue the lost and the common good. Such churches intentionally practice public faith in order to affect biblical culture transformation as they bear faithful witness to the kingdom reality of God's rule in human affairs. "The church, having received the Spirit of baptism at Pentecost, became the prophetic community empowered for the missionary task." [4] The Holy Spirit infused the people of God with the same transforming power that energized the life and ministry of Jesus and raised Him from the dead (Eph. 1:19–20).

God desires to manifest this power for new life through His church (4:3–4). The *missio Dei* unity—flowing from the Father, through the Son (John 17:22–23) by the Holy Spirit, and into the church (14:16–17)—bears witness to God's kingdom, not just on earth, but also to the rulers and authorities in the heavenly realms (Eph. 3:10). It proclaims the eternal reconciliation purpose that God has accomplished through Christ. The redeemed church cannot manifest this resurrection power without supernatural assistance. So, Christ apportions gifts to his church and enables believers for works of service (1 Cor. 12:4–11) to bring God's benevolent purposes in all sectors of society.

God modeled His preferred *modus operandi* in the incarnation of Jesus. He was fully God and fully human, yet one person. Although the church is not on the same level as Jesus, it carries a similar incarnational nature. At the point where the supernatural (all of God) meets the natural (all of man), the gifts begin. [5] In this way, God the Spirit helps the church do for God's Kingdom what it cannot do by itself. If believers consider both the Lukan and the Pauline conceptions of Pentecost together, they will see Christ equipped the church with the power to witness, with spiritual gifts and with a divine pattern of government (Eph. 4:11–13). [6] Committed Christians to the *missio Dei* understand the Father and the Son sent the Holy Spirit to empower the church for its kingdom witness in the world. The New Testament identifies the church's mission with that of the Kingdom of God—the divine realm where God's representatives act on His behalf and establish the reign of God's effective will. In that capacity, the church becomes God's Kingdom witness.

On Their Turf

The Kingdom of God does not confine itself to a specific geographical location. The church's role in the reconciliation mission is to bear witness to the invisible Kingdom of God through faithful Christian living in all spheres of society, so God the Father can rescue sinners from the domain of darkness and bring them into the Kingdom of His Son (Acts 26:18). The gospel of Christ is still the gospel of the Kingdom (Matt. 4:23), the good news of righteousness, peace, and joy in the Holy Spirit.

As we discussed in the previous chapters, effective culture-reaching gospel-sharing in the twenty-first century does not happen on our turf or terms. That is why Churches for Monday are proactively integrating their faith into the marketplace. Since we are the gospel incarnate (2 Cor. 3:3), we have to be ready to go instead of wait for people to come. The architectural allure of a rooftop steeple or a cross is captivating less and less to our postmodern, post-Christian neighbors. The latest statistics show only 38 percent of Christians are active churchgoers . [7] There is nothing wrong in having architectural artifacts on our buildings, or religious rituals in our services, but in some parts of the country, these now are alienating instead of reaching people.

The Good News is still good news, and it works in all domains, so it is safe to walk it outside of our church walls. Nothing from the potency of the reconciliation message will be lost. We'll even gain something—an informed way to translate the gospel so the unchurched can hear and thoughtfully consider it. This news of hope is potable and tangible and deserves to be integrated into work, economics, and entrepreneurship. What we believers simply need to do can turn out being difficult to do. Since you are a thoughtful Christian, you already know that. I hope the practical ways I'm offering throughout the book to prepare for mission on Monday will be helpful to you.

The Barna study, "Christians at Work," shows that only 26 percent of believers strongly agree when they go to work what they do at their jobs is serving God or a higher purpose.[8] The rest have a hard time clearly seeing how their faith integrates into their work to display the image of Creator God to an unbelieving world. Most still struggle to realize that their potential in serving God in the workplace is not determined by how sacred or well-suited the work environment becomes to our faith, but rather how well our faith in God becomes integrated into what we do at work.

Kingdom Integrators

All things are not lost. Barna research identifies a group of Christians whom they call "Integrators" that not only clearly sees how the work they are doing is serving God and a higher purpose, but also finds purpose and meaning in the work they do. They are Christians who believe it is important to help mold the culture of their workplace to make a difference in the world. [9] These Integrators amount to an estimated 28 percent of all Christians in the workforce. "There are men and women who sit in our pews who walk into board meetings, classrooms, warehouses, and offices and interact with clients with a deep sense that God is there and that God is up to something in this world. They are teachers, lawyers, executives, ditch diggers, non-profit leaders, social workers, and health care professionals who have developed a sense that their work is not simply something to endure, but it's the very place they experience God's presence and transforming power. They see their work not as a means to an end—that is, a place to find people to bring to church; they see their work as the location where healing begins and God's Kingdom comes near." [10]

This type of witness is imperative for the transformation of our work environments plagued by greed, selfishness, bigotry, division, and hatred. The Integrators see their faith as the foundation of their identity, and they require more of themselves as workers and as people of faith. They have a growth mindset, are entrepreneurial—embracing curiosity and risk, and use their gifts and talents at work so they can glorify God and mold the culture of their workplace[11]—their sphere of influence.

If you are part of the Kingdom-witnessing Integrators or want to join them, you are on the front line, leading the way for the church to follow. Be encouraged the Spirit will continually give you strength to add value to the lives of others by being compassionate, resourceful, gentle, patient, and hardworking. Your weekday witness testifies to a loving God who offers abundant life as He intended it. You are doing a significant, full time ministry work outside of the church walls in a vocation that doesn't require preaching in the pulpit, but instead in the marketplace.

Encouraging Work as Worship

God reigns in human affairs in the Redeeming Work of Jesus Christ who came to destroy the works of the Devil." [12] Although, the Kingdom of justice and *shalom* will arrive in its fullness only at the return of King Jesus, believers cannot afford to lapse into passive inactivity in the marketplace, because the church exemplifies that reign, and its main role is to build a Sunday-to-Monday connect bridge to the divine grace available to people.

Yet, Barna identifies a big group of Christians (72 percent) as Compartmentalizers and Onlookers. The Compartmentalizers make up 34 percent of pragmatic employees without strong connections to their faith or work.[13] "Just one in ten Compartmentalizers (11% vs. 77% of Integrators) feels called to or made for their current work. Even more revealing: One in five Compartmentalizers (22%) says they have never even thought about whether their calling and career overlap (vs. 6% of Integrators). . . . Generally, Compartmentalizers seem to concentrate on what they can earn, rather than spiritually contribute, in employment." [14] The Onlookers make up 38 percent of passive employees positioned to better connect with their faith and work. [15] These are the workers moderately interested in the world around them (38% strongly agree). The Barna Group suggests that one can think of the Onlookers in two ways: as apathetic or stagnant, or as potential Integrators whose vocational passion has not yet been refined or released. And although the Onlookers are not overly eager to shape the culture of their workplace (only 20 percent consider that to be "completely" important), "this is something they could be spurred toward, as 58 percent still call it 'somewhat' important" and their responses suggest good intentions and latent gifts. [16]

The high number of seventy two percent of semi- or inactive Christians in the workforce who don't fully connect the importance of their faith to their mission at work gives basis for concern. We have to strategically prepare believers on Sunday for work on Monday by teaching them that joining Jesus in His work in the marketplace constitutes the very core of every redeemed life. I believe many Christians desire to be Integrators, or can be awakened to it, if church leaders regularly affirm Monday work is as important as Sunday work and help them see what they do at their jobs as worship and blessing. While believers await the kingdom's full consummation, we must enact and embody foretastes of the coming realities of that Kingdom right where we work. It is awe-inspiring that Jesus' disciples had the privilege of participating in His work of redemption. As followers of Jesus, that privilege and responsibility is also extended to you and me. Are you ready to reignite your vocational passion and integrate your faith into everything you do?

Apostolic DNA

The apostolic function should form the core DNA of the Church for Monday. Throughout history, the *missio Dei* has compelled the people of God to sound a call for transformation amidst the nations. God still sends His church to be the salt and the light in the twenty-first-century postmodern culture—in its schools, corporations, parks, TV stations, art galleries, halls of justice, and government. Jesus gave a comprehensive picture of His charge to all believers (John 17:17–20). He promised the miraculous signs that marked His work would also follow all who have faith in Him (14:12). He commissioned the original apostles and all future believers with the task to represent the triune God among a perishing world: "As you sent (*apostellō*) me into the world, I have sent (*apostellō*) them into the world" (17:18).

Although the apostolic witness stands uniquely in authenticating New Testament Christianity, witnessing to Christ went beyond the apostles. "All following generations of believers were enlisted in the ongoing task of bearing witness to the same Lord Jesus Christ, in whom they had come to believe through the apostolic witness."[17] To be apostolic is to be as committed as God's Apostle Son was to carrying out the mission of the Father. [18] The Father sent the Son as a missionary to the world, to bring the world back to God. In like fashion, the *missio Dei* continues through a frail, yet forgiven, twenty-first-century missionary church that is sent to bear witness in its own backyard, right outside of its church walls.

Incarnational Hope

The gospel of the Kingdom is powerful because it is divine yet incarnate. "The Word became flesh and blood and moved into the neighborhood" (John 1:14, *The Message*), and modeled holiness to all humanity as a normative lifestyle. Now the Spirit-empowered church functions among depraved communities and continues the holiness standard, since Kingdom living doesn't conform to sinful life patterns, but offers the world a counter-cultural value system (1 Pet. 1:13–16). To be an incarnational model of hope, a church that equips for Monday must move from traditional, church-centric practices to adopt a missional stance. Only in this way will it serve as God's catalyst for transformation in the marketplace.

Churches that bridge Sunday worship to Monday work display God's hope, goodness, justice, opportunity, and creativity, as they treat their coworkers, employees, and bosses with kindness and respect, elevate human dignity, seize creative opportunities and take risks, in order to find solutions to problems in engineering, architecture, construction, education, forestry, and other industries. They become an incarnational witness and a blessing, as they have been blessed by God with wisdom, knowledge, and understanding, thus ushering God's purposes and solutions from heaven to earth for the common good. Just as "He causes his sun to rise on the evil and the good, and sends rain on the righteous and the unrighteous" (Matt. 5:45b).

A Catalyst of Transformation

Jesus' incarnation not only initiated God's redemptive purposes, but it also provided a model for transformational ministry. Some people reject the gospel not because they perceive it to be *false*, but because they perceive it to be *trivial*. "They are looking for an integrated worldview that makes sense of all their experience."[19] That is why, if contemporary Christians live out their faith in the midst of a broken culture filled with scarcity, drugs, homelessness, illiteracy, adultery, divorce, child molestation, pornography, and the like, they can steward their presence by becoming catalysts of transformation. The proper response to the grace of God is for the church to enter into the pain and suffering of the people of its neighborhoods and the people in the workforce through proximity, relationships, solidarity, and humility.

In pursuit of biblical expression of ministry, churches that desire to serve their communities send believers outside the four walls of their buildings to under-resourced neighborhoods. The Lord promised, "If you spend yourselves in behalf of the hungry and satisfy the needs of the oppressed, then your light will rise in the darkness, and your night will become like the noonday" (Isa. 58:10). Also, by seeking to restore broken environments in the public arena, believers obey God's will and unlock the potential for lasting community transformation.

When the local church affirms the unique contribution every believer makes through their spiritual and natural gifts as lawyers, builders, baristas, architects, seamstresses, doctors, teachers, construction workers—and many others—then it brings the effective reign of Jesus in their own neighborhoods and workforce and model a redeemed way of living. Humans are hardwired for imitation. The church serves as a model to a lost world. As followers of Jesus we are to engage in the spiritual and material transformation of our cities by prayerfully seeking its peace and prosperity, because living in community means that our neighbors' plight is like our own. Living life deeply ingrained in the local neighborhood is the key not only to changing the unchurched community, but the Christian one as well. If the favor of God prospers our neighbors, then we, too, prosper by enjoying community full of God's joy, innovation, justice, kindness, and opportunity for all (Jer. 29:7).

A Real-Life Story—Economically Developing the Marginalized in the Marketplace

How many leaders do we have sitting in our own congregations? Within the walls of the church there is a great emphasis on spiritual development. Programs are filled with biblical teachings on discipleship, core values, prayer, fasting, etc. Learning about the spiritual aspects of Christianity is vital to any believer. Is the church meeting the needs of their community by investing in a holistic change? A holistic change is a change that happens socially, spiritually, and economically. Striving to transform the whole life of an individual not only affects them, but also the community as well. Pastor Fernando Tamara of Orange County First Assembly of God Church (OCFA) in Santa Ana, California, understands the significance of integrating spiritual growth with opportunities for people to grow socially in a community and economically through work. Here is OCFA Church's story shared with me by Pastor Fernando Tamara in a written interview.

> It began with preaching that God intends for all people to flourish," says Tamara who pastors OCFA's Spanish-speaking campus.

> This biblical truth—that God intends for all people to flourish—resonated with Jose, an immigrant from Latin America. He came to the church because he had a relationship with a young lady who attends OCFA. Jose comes from a broken family, and sadly, he came to the church with no vision and paralyzed by fear.

> Jose is not the only Latin American immigrant paralyzed by fear. "In Santa Ana, it takes longer for Latino immigrants to be enculturated," laments Tamara. "One reason for this is that many who migrate from Latin America consider oppression, poverty, and injustice as normative. Because

they believe the American majority culture will oppress them, they hesitate to learn the English language or assimilate into the American culture."

However, Jose mustered up enough courage to request a meeting with Tamara and said, "I notice you speak a lot about God intending for all persons to blossom or flourish. I want that. Would you pray that I find a job?" It was not too long after that Jose landed a job at a pool cleaning business.

Jose arrived at OCFA with no vision for his life. However, after working for several years with a pool cleaning business, Jose developed a vision to own his own pool cleaning business. Again, he approached Tamara and shared his vision to be a business owner. Tamara knew that aspiring entrepreneurs need financial capital and social capital. Tamara called three church members—a marketing professional, a cleaning company professional, and a financial advisor to meet with Tamara and Jose. This was an opportunity for Tamara to facilitate what he calls "exchange of service and wisdom." These professionals shared with Jose lessons learned, best practices, and pitfalls to avoid.

Jose got inspired to become a legal US citizen and also to pass a challenging pool inspector test that many fail the first time. In America, Jose learned that having pool inspector credentials equates to having credibility as a business owner. Today Jose is a pool cleaning business owner. His clientele includes customers from OCFA's English and Spanish speaking congregations, and he is now producing value for the local economy. Business is going so well that he is looking to hire someone from the church to be his assistant.

Jose's transformation from having *no vision* to having *an economic vision* commenced with Tamara's preaching on human flourishing and the work of the Holy Spirit. Relationally and organically, Tamara invested in Jose's life and soon became his confidante and prayer partner.

Tamara's hands-on discipling and access to social capital coupled with Jose's economic vision catapulted him to launching his own business." [20]

"The spirit empowers us daily to resemble Christ," Tamara says. "He is reflected in everything we do, including our work." Tamara's church has a whole-life-discipleship model that strategizes to pair marketplace veterans with visionary leaders from the church. "When we have a large group of retired professionals who come to church every week and we avoid engaging them in this conversation, we have neglected one of the most important characteristics of human beings: sharing our narrative."

Tamara's example encourages us to continue socio-economic ministry that closes the Sunday-to-Monday gap, and in this way lifts our congregations spiritually, socially, and economically.

Invested in Cultural Transformation

Belong Before Believe

You may have heard the phrase "belong before believe." That phrase had grazed my ears in the past, but I had not paid attention to it until I was training to become a church planter. Belong before believe means a person is welcomed into a group, like a church, participates in that group, and gains a sense of belonging prior to fully embracing what the group believes. None of the churches I belonged to as a member, or led as a pastor, talked about "belong before believe." Now I was starting the exciting journey of church startup, and my training church-planting boot camps were full of catchy slogans like that. "Belong before believe" especially appealed to me because it seemed to suit the culture we were going to build at Real Life Church. I had dreamt about starting a church embedded in the economy of our city that would incubate businesses, teach essential entrepreneurial skills, and foster next-generation creativity. My team and I were going to open our doors to "whosoever," because we were going to work as "salt and light" among the unchurched business community and some might want to belong to a faith community before they fully embraced its belief system. Hence, we adopted the slogan "belong before believe."

Although trained in church startup and formally educated in leadership and theology, I did not anticipate half of what this innovative, Holy Spirit-inspired prototype of church was going to teach me about discipleship. Christian faith is about transformation of the whole life. People have to change what they believe so they can change the way they live. This is the essence of the gospel. As church planters, my team and I found ourselves becoming culture-transformation agents because, for the most part, we were working among de-churched and unchurched people.

We began discipling our unchurched friends by offering leadership training, business workshops, and entrepreneurial meetups—programs seemingly secular in theme, but not in principle. We taught core biblical values by teaching such things as leading well by practicing servant leadership, doing just business by ensuring just wages, elevating human dignity at work by honoring both the employees and their bosses, caring for the marginalized by training them in job skills and job searches. Those who stuck around began to consider some of these new principles of doing life, and eventually, were open to considering Jesus.

The years of pastoring an organic church startup (a church started without relying on Christians transferring from other churches) that has seen many salvations taught me there is nothing more exciting than a personal transformation. Also, there is nothing more slow, messy, and non-linear than a personal transformation. Old ways and beliefs take time to surface, be recognized, and then surrendered to God. A person's formation into the image of Christ is not about speed, but about perseverance. Doing church in the marketplace required me and my team not just novel model of church, but a good understanding of culture-making, and unwavering commitment to culture formation. These new believers agreed to embrace the belief system Jesus modeled and taught, and now they were making it their own. In short, when people say yes to Jesus, they are saying yes to a complete overhaul of culture.

When changing cultures, it is not only about the beginning, but about the process that brings the product of transformation to fruition. Can a person stick with the daily "taking off" the old culture and "putting on" the new one (Ephesians 4:22b-24) without waning conviction and with compelling consistency? When church planters, pastors, and lay leaders work with the unchurched, they do the work of culture transformation guides. This work is richly rewarding and deeply challenging, transforming the pastor as much as it is transforming his or her unchurched friend.

To guide people in culture transformation is one of the most rigorous commitments believers make as they embrace the Great Commission. When the church takes seriously to building spaces of belonging for our neighbors before they embrace what we believe, often that means we will invest many hours in shaping relationships with those who don't act or think like we do. That time may seem wasted because our touches with the unchurched will not quickly convert into Sunday morning attendance, filled-in conversion cards, or water baptisms. Welcome to the life of a church starter! Today church planting has many fans from afar, and it is often looked upon as this "sexy" thing some pastors are doing. There is nothing sexy, comfortable, or easy in starting churches; only long hours of prayer, multifaceted work, and low paychecks. Yet one of the highest forms of joy on earth is having a front row seat at culture transformation. Although we are not all called to be church planters, we can find a part in the endeavor if we are willing to enter the marketplace for the long haul and make space for people to belong, so they may consider the good news about Jesus Christ and believe.

Theological Underpinnings for Culture Transformation

Paul warned the Roman church, "Do not conform any longer to the pattern of this world but be transformed by the renewing of your mind" (Rom. 12:2). People reject God's authority, defining good and evil within their own unregenerate beings. Sinful culture rejects the gospel message and Christian worldview because its core assumptions form in the kingdom of darkness.

Biblical transformation will always be both individual and social. Every human being has a personal culture and is an active culture maker of a social group—a subset of a larger culture. This is why biblical transformation begins with the change of a person's culture, from a condition of human existence lived contrary to God's creation purpose, to a condition full of life in harmony with God (Col. 3:8–10). Although biblical transformation begins with the individual, it does not end there. The result of the *missio Dei* is transformed individuals, joining transformed communities (churches), to form transformed cultures. Read that again—individuals, then communities, then culture. Too often the church wants to begin with culture, but that is not the way this works.

At the moment of salvation, the Holy Spirit baptizes the individual into the corporate body of Christ (1 Cor. 12:13), which influences the individual toward spiritual growth. The individual is not inactive, but in turn, influences the corporate body. New believers add their spiritual gifts and natural talents, as well as give fresh eyes to the church community, and this in turn helps mature believers connect with the unchurched culture in more compelling ways to make disciples in the marketplace. In this continued culture formation, the church community helps new believers to walk out their new identity, with resilience and commitment, while new believers help those in the church better understand the pain points of current unchurched cultures.

This exchange of cultures is supernatural, yet, in full cooperation with the individual. "Taking off" the old self and "putting on" the new requires sacrifice and suffering. Following Jesus is about denying to oneself, because we are willingly giving up what we have known and practiced about the world. Now, as new believers, we are to take off the ways we thought and acted, and put on the ways of Jesus. This sacrificial daily abandoning of one's old culture, in order to fully adopt and not just semi-adapt to a new way of living, is the battle of the soul we lead from the day we say 'yes' to Jesus and 'no' to the ways of the fallen world in which we live. Therefore, when entering the public arena to make disciples, we should approach people with the humble realization that we are asking them to make a costly decision to overhaul their lives (Luke 14:25–34).

Every community has a culture, or at least a subculture, with its core beliefs that define it. Edgar Schein, a leading expert in social science and organizational culture, asserts any group's culture can be studied at three levels: (1) artifacts, (2) espoused values, and (3) underlying core beliefs and assumptions. [1] Like an iceberg, a culture shows only its tip, the observable artifacts, and espoused values. The underlying core beliefs most often are difficult to discern; they are the subconscious principles that guide people's actions. But change in culture primarily occurs by transforming its underlying assumptions—the core belief system. This is neither an easy, nor a fast task because these deeply seated subconscious principles keep resurfacing every time life throws us a curveball and we reach out to the old paradigms of solving problems. For example, we become anxious when we are facing difficulties because we fall back to the old ways we had when we lived without Jesus. We become bitter when we are wronged, because, although saved by grace, we haven't mastered giving grace to others. This is why not forsaking the gathering of believers, but doing life in transformed communities as Christians (Heb. 10:25) is not just a good idea, but an essential lifeline. Culture is formed person to person, peer group to peer group, as "iron sharpens iron, so one person sharpens another" (Prov. 27:17), supporting each other to live life as God intended.

Jesus placed His church in the world (John 17:18) and gave it the charge to epitomize the life-preserving properties of salt (Matt. 5:13–14). Worldly cultures transform under the influence of the Holy Spirit and the witness of the church—a counter-culture society that practices kingdom principles, which challenge the fundamental values of godless cultures. Throughout history, the triune God has formed a witnessing people who accept the Creator-creature distinction—acknowledging there is only one God, and we are not Him— and live an existence contingent upon God's provision. First in Israel, and now in the church, God's people offer the world an alternative worldview and behavior paradigm that subjects itself to divine wisdom. God is not just saving individuals and preparing them for heaven; rather, He is creating a *people* among whom He can live and who in their life together will reproduce God's life and character. [2] God works in His people in order to work through His people in the world.

In the World, Not of the World

Only God-inspired values of light can build human cultures on justice, mercy, and love; these are the characteristics of the triune culture. Unfortunately, Christians typically break or lose their ties with unbelievers as they enter their new church family, removing the Sunday-to-Monday Connect Bridge that can reach worldly cultures. They have taken Jesus' "not of this world" commission as literal separation from society, consequently diminishing the witness of godly core beliefs in the marketplace. Jesus calls His church to be separate in the way He is separate, by worldview and practice, not by physical space and church-centric ministries.

Not supporting secular worldviews is not enough to transform culture. The church in America has often found it easier to yell, picket, or disagree with culture, and to critique, condemn, or criticize culture. This type of engagement in no way has lessened the deeply polarized belief systems of our society. Now it has become infinitely more difficult for the church to shape culture in the public square. We have a kingdom mandate to live lives that thoughtfully challenge the unregenerate values of our society, and actively and imaginatively work toward Christian culture formation.

It is imperative believers work toward becoming culture makers once again. If the church stays active within its postmodern communities, it will earn a place in the public arena to negotiate its culture's values and underlying core beliefs. Reaching out to broken humanity is not just the duty of vocational evangelists, or of missionaries who dedicate their lives to Christian service abroad. Extending compassion and capacity to the lost is the essential reason for the church's existence: to be salt and light, presenting Christ as the "hope of glory" to perishing cultures (Col. 1:27). That salt and light exposes and heals depravity, it invites sinners to repentance and a change of belief systems. While evil still wreaks havoc throughout the creation, Christians can bear witness to the loving, just rule of God by modeling the life of the age to come in the present. [3]

When believers are deeply embedded in their environments, they can become culture makers in the public arena. Ed Silovoso, a contemporary marketplace minister, points to that culture formation potential: "Today millions of men and women are called to full-time ministry in business, education, and government—the marketplace. They can do more than witness; they can bring transformation to their jobs and then to their cities—as happened in the first century." [4]

Reaching Out to Diverse Cultures

People in all cultures are in desperate need of a Savior, yet most despise the witness of the counter-cultural community of the people of God because it exposes their depraved way of thinking and need for change. Culture's responses may vary, from outright rejection of the idea that God even exists, to repentance and rejection of their sinful core beliefs.

Not all world cultures will transform into Christian communities until the consummation of times, [5] but societies that recognize the monotheistic, triune rule have seen both moral and material growth since the first human community in the Garden of Eden. Presently, a third of the world's population is Christian.[6] In partnership with Yahweh, the people of God have the potential to influence all spheres of societies' life, taking steps in aligning human existence with God's creation purposes.

For most people, the journey to God is a long one. Jesus did not rush people to make a profession of faith, as many of us would like to do. I often have to remind myself to be patient when giving altar calls because many newcomers do not understand the invitation to grace and salvation unless they have been around church for some time. On more than one occasion, I have led people to a decision for Christ and a salvation experience in a one-on-one conversation after a service because they needed more time and clarity to process what they are committing to. Notably, Jesus asked His listeners to count the cost of following His supreme authority that they might successfully finish the journey (Luke 14:25–33). Even though the born again experience happens instantaneously, sanctified living is a process that moves the believer along towards ever increasing likeness to God. The decision to exchange one's dissolute existence for righteous living in Christ presupposes gospel-and-God-awareness, which in turn demands thoughtful consideration.

The transformation process of cultures is interrupted throughout history and often spirals downward. From the opening chapters of Genesis, throughout the period of the Judges, Israel's monarchy, and all the way through today's postmodernism, the human continuum responds in depravity. Yet, in God's redemptive act of continually reaching out to cultures, transformation becomes possible. God has purposed to reach out to human cultures before the creation of the world. He chose Christ as His instrument of mission, and through His representatives, the *people* of God, He continually offers grace to all humanity.

Missio Dei's goal extends beyond individualized soul-winning to effecting culture transformation. The church has grasped the significance of individual salvation, but often does not intentionally pursue groups of people and entire cultures. An effective missional approach must include corporate influence on a culture.

A Real-Life Story—Contextualizing the Gospel in Public Spaces

Providencia Church translates the essence of the gospel message and looks for the seat at the table in the marketplace of their city in order to reach the unchurched. Here is Providencia Church's story shared with me by Pastor Keith Case in a written interview.

> Providencia was born in West Palm Beach, Florida out of what's known in the counseling world as a process group. A concept similar to this, coined by Dan Allender in his book, *To Be Told*, is a Story Group. Story Groups are an integral part of the framework of our church, and we use them to welcome people into a space of vulnerability and true connection. The grace of God provides freedom to explore our own stories, even amongst the greatest wounds and tragedies. Our church's history magnifies the name, 'Providencia,' which was a ship in the late 1800s that grounded on the shore of Palm Beach, spilled its cargo of coconuts, and created a colony of palm trees that eventually led to the planting of West Palm Beach.

> We do not own a place for worship or for our offices. We rent space from a church on Sunday nights. During the week, the staff and I meet with people in local businesses and spaces around the city for story groups and exploration groups, with an intention of listening to the needs and dreams of West Palm Beach's residents. We are a community of priests who believe we have been called, above all else, to listen to our city. Out of these efforts we have been invited to partner with private and governmental organizations to help unearth the city's soul.

One of the initiatives born out of this work is UniverCity. As a non-profit, UniverCity connects local artists, businesses, and civic leaders in various work sectors to put on educational classes from finances and entrepreneurship to the arts and health. In the same vein, the church's worship team created Paradise Hymns, a collective of members that writes music echoing our desire to see God's Kingdom come in West Palm Beach.

In many ways, we are a community of artists. Out of a congregation of 120 people, you'll find four to five poets, over ten actors and writers, four to five dancers, and around ten unique bands. We have sought to embrace those who can be found on the margins of society and those without a faith background. The long term vision that God has given us is to welcome the city's residents out of their own personal Egypt, out of shame and hiding, and into freedom in Christ. Part of this journey is helping people see how the Gospel applies not just to their personal lives, but to their neighborhoods and industries, too.

PART THREE

FRUITFUL
APPLICATION

The Scorecard

An Example to Follow

W. E. H. Lecky says the moral influence of Jesus' teachings on the Western world was the most powerful moral lever that has ever been applied to the affairs of man. [1] This new way of life challenged all human cultures. In this present age, we see only partial transformation; neither all world cultures nor every person in a group culture will align with the authority of King Jesus before the Second Coming. Nevertheless, among those that accept His reign, the Spirit of God forms a transformed community, which in turn goes on to transform societies. Thus, the church becomes a sign, symbol, and foretaste of God's redeeming love in real neighborhoods, bearing witness to a new way of being human.

Jesus continuously challenged the religious leaders of His day to understand the Law was not given to restrict people in their basic tasks, but to encourage them to live in harmony with one another and with God. Twenty-one centuries later, the challenge to church leaders remains the same—answer in love. When going after the Great Commission, do not forget the Great Commandment. A church that is preparing to embed itself in the marketplace for culture formation, needs to be transformed itself and pay close attention to the attitude of the heart, because this is what ultimately matters. We must love our neighbor, as Jesus loved us—from the heart and till the end (John 13:34). If we only do outreach programs for the sake of our scorecard then we are not doing it for the sake of our neighbor. Before we reach sinful people outside the church let's make them a place to belong with forgiven people inside the church. Let's remember justification depends on the mercy of God to the repentant and not on the works of the repentant. When Zacchaeus restored his ill-gotten gains, this did not precede but followed his acceptance by Jesus (Luke 19:1–10).

Chances are none of us got into leadership in order to see our churches stop reaching new people and stop accomplishing God's mission. But almost every church in our Western culture is challenged to navigate the new trends of a post-Christian society. For churches who realize new times call for new methods, I suggest we re-envision Jesus' first-century method for today's twenty-first-century church. As we are revamping our churches track-record, can we do it by keeping in mind the three *S's* Jesus practiced regularly (Luke 19:1-10)?

- Seek

- See

- Sit

Jesus went out to *seek* the lost in the middle of their marketplace activities. Of the 52 parables Jesus told, 45 had a workplace context. [2] Jesus himself spent His adult life in the profession of a carpenter. It is in the marketplace where He was able to see Peter and Andrew, James and John, Zacchaeus, Levi, the centurion, the woman at the well, and so many others. Then He joined them to sit at their table to listen to their brokenness in order to offer His redeeming solution to their pain. No wonder so many who felt outcasts felt they belonged in Jesus' company.

What if our church activities centered on the priorities Jesus centered His on, so we can see results Jesus saw? Seek out the marketplace Zacchaeuses as Jesus did, see them as Jesus did, sit at their table as Jesus did, *before* they believe and repent, as Zacchaeus did.

In an experience-oriented, high-touch, post-truth world, where many look for spirituality, but not Christianity, the Holy Spirit empowers the church to contextualize its witness for cultural application. The spiritual climate in North America and the West allows for many religious thoughts to exist together. If in this new landscape local churches **seek** out their communities, by familiarizing themselves with their pains and joys, **see** the people and people groups affected by brokenness, and **sit** at the community's table not as "the know it all," but as "I want to hear it all," in order to gain society's ear, then they'll be able to bridge the Sunday-to-Monday gap. They'll get the response that Zacchaeus gave— repent and believe. If we assume the humble posture of an explorer of the marketplace, then we can revamp the church's focus to reflect the heart of God for our postmodern neighbor.

The Scorecard

It is not possible to unpack the depth of the scorecard for the Church for Monday in one chapter. This topic deserves an entire book. Here I will outline with broad strokes some important points about what to measure and how to measure the components of the scorecard in order to begin the conversation.

When talking about the scorecard, there is a question to consider: "Are you willing to shift from church-centric scorecard to kingdom-centric scorecard?" And another important one: "Are you willing to expand what you celebrate?" Unless we see the value of measuring impact beyond the Sunday gathering, we won't be willing to envision new ways of what and how we measure.

Most churches have a scorecard which measures how well our congregations do on Sunday and not how well our congregants do on Monday. This has to change if we want to change how well the church does in the marketplace. Not only do we have to connect Sunday to Monday, but we need to bring Monday back to Sunday. What I mean is the gathered experience on Sunday needs to focus on equipping believers for the scattered Monday mission, which is to oversee how God's kingdom shows up on earth in our own communities amidst societal ills.

The church is present in the world not to build itself but to build the kingdom of God in the marketplace and to bring people into a life-giving experience with King Jesus. We are commissioned to steward God's redeeming presence for our communities. When whole-life disciples embedded in the economy prayerfully seek God's wisdom at work while solving a financial crisis with a client, or offer an innovative design that has stumped the creative team, or mitigate in a peaceful manner amidst a high-strung, nerve-wracking case that ushers God's kingdom and redeeming presence and translates the gospel for the unchurched by conveying Christ's love to them. Jesus was sharply focused on the kingdom of God. During His earthly ministry, He talked about the kingdom of God and the kingdom of heaven over 100 times and only once about the church on the backdrop of the kingdom of heaven. [3] Our scorecard must reflect how the church expands the territories of God's kingdom in the marketplace or it won't have the right parameters. The role of the local church and every function it does is pivotal for the life of the community because it ushers in the kingdom of God as the source of all life. Nothing can substitute that role and the foretaste it brings. No social services, government programs, or civil groups can restore the broken lives in our communities as does the King of the heavenly kingdom that works through His church anywhere the church engages the life of the community. For that reason it is imperative we get outside of our church-centric bubble and connect to the marketplace in meaningful ways to bring to it the fullness of life as Jesus intended people to have.

Pastors, we are entrusted with Jesus' flock to equip them for the majority, not just the minority, of their life wherever it takes them outside of the church walls. Will you join me in recalibrating our church's scorecard to reflect the biblical conviction of whole-life discipleship both as a gathered and a scattered church, bringing the Kingdom of God amidst a broken marketplace?

Beyond the 3 Bs: Bodies, Bucks, and Buildings

Regardless of what else makes the list of a church's parameters, and how intentional, or lapsed the church is in measuring results, three things are ever present on any church's scorecard—the 3 Bs: Bodies, Bucks, and Buildings. The question is: "Are these parameters sufficient for the Church for Monday Scorecard, or should we go beyond them?" Since measuring church success has always revolved around those three (sometimes expressed as the church's ABCs— Attendance, Buildings, and Cash), how much do they matter? Are they the "holy trinity" for a local church? Kind of, yes.

Before you start throwing rocks and scriptures at me, you should know I am the last person to be taken over by practicality. I usually function in a big-picture capacity, focused on trends and seeing future realities decades before they happen. Details like how many people it will take to achieve the vision and how much money it will cost usually come second to me. But not to my MBA-trained husband, who stewards millions of dollars through his marketplace vocation and is detail-oriented in personality. To him, all of my church-dreaming has always translated into bodies, bucks, and buildings. In God's providential wisdom, I am partnered with someone who keeps the practical side of things on the front burner. So, I understand the need for strong numbers of bodies, bucks, and buildings. Without a comprehensive vision of biblically faithful, theologically informed, and missionally aligned 3Bs, we will be stuck in the red with the accounting books. Measuring matters, but what we measure and why we measure it matters more.

What do we measure? We need to define the *it*, or we will never hit it. I tell the entrepreneurs I business-consult, unless they have a clear vision of their future enterprise and then reverse-engineer a pathway to it, they will never get there. When an entrepreneur starts a business, they must picture the mature business in full, then chart a path to it with obtainable and measurable first and next steps that lead to their desired destination, not to someone else's. Otherwise, their startup is only going to confirm the statistic that 90 percent of small businesses fail in the first five years."[4] Vision is also important to the pastor and the success of their church. Without a God-breathed, clear vision for the church's DNA—its unique place in the global body of Christ, growth structure, and supporting systems—the local church may also find itself becoming a grim statistic.

Let's envision the future of the church so we can reverse-engineer a pathway to it. The *it* is a church embedded in the marketplace, making not only a lasting spiritual, but also a socio-economic difference, as well. This type of vision cannot be measured with a church-centric scorecard. That scorecard is only concerned with how well the congregation is doing on Sunday but hasn't expanded its categories to measure how well the congregants do on Monday. A new kingdom-centric scorecard is needed to measure how the gathered experience prepares the scattered church for mission at work and the practice of whole-life discipleship.

In addition to the gathered experience, measuring and celebrating impact beyond Sunday is what the revamped scorecard must reflect. Measuring the 3Bs for your scattered church marketplace impact, the Sunday-to-Monday Connect Bridge, and Integration Onramps must garner the same passion and adequate budget as measuring the 3Bs for Sunday.

This is only a segment of what comprises our Real Life Scorecard but this offers a glimpse of the priorities we measure:

Bodies:

- Salvations
- Water Baptisms
- Miraculous physical healings
- Households ministered through church services
- Unchurched households reached Monday to Sunday
- Sunday guests co-workers of church members
- Employment opportunity assistance of church families
- Upward mobility of church families
- Increased revenue of the Real Life Entrepreneurs
- Scaled businesses of the Real Life Entrepreneurs
- Entrepreneurs ministered through the entrepreneurial center
- Kids ministered through the entrepreneurial youth programs
- Teens ministered through the entrepreneurial youth programs
- Local pastors and Christian entrepreneurs equipped for marketplace ministry

Budget:

- Tithes, offerings, rental space and additional creative revenue steams
- Scholarships for kids and teens entrepreneurial youth programs

- Fund-raising for faith-based entrepreneurial training

Building:

Networking events, business meetups, community workshops, financial training, private offices, co-working space, event space, retreats.

What are your priorities that your church's scorecard measures? Since we defined the *it* to be a church embedded in the marketplace, let's envision it. When reverse-engineering a vision the following elements are key:

- Envision the mature vision

It is important that we envision in full, as much as we can master, the mature and not the infancy stage of an endeavor, in order to shoot at that target. The mature endeavor is our "there." Pray about it—Spirit-inspired visons are the key to our success. Then do your research and write down as many details as you can.

For example, the bull's eye of our Real Life marketplace church is developing thriving multiple cities in the U.S. and abroad by developing their entrepreneurs. What is your dream of the marketplace in your city?

When my team and I envisioned what God was inspiring us toward we saw a multi-site church embedded in the economy, translating the gospel for the unchurched, and equipping whole-life disciples to expand God's kingdom and its presence in the marketplace. But we could never get there if we didn't chart the path to it.

- Chart a path

The path connects our "here" to our "there." It is helpful if the path is penned on paper. Our brains process and retain well visual maps. Since we've already defined our "there," we need to realistically assess the present situation of our "here" in order to envision what road to take and what steps to put in place.

- Define obtainable and measurable first steps

Your first steps are important. You usually have several preparatory steps to take to position you for a successful transition from where you are to get on the road heading to there. Be realistic about your time and resources as you chart the steps and give yourself and your church obtainable timelines to achieve them. Otherwise, you'll get discouraged fast and likely to decide that becoming a marketplace-embedded church wasn't a good idea.

• Define obtainable and measurable next steps

Your next steps keep the momentum going. Unfortunately, after the initial steps, many entrepreneurs run out of steam and their endeavors crash, because the excitement of the newness wears off and all that's left is hard work. Birthing a new venture is a costly endeavor—it will require resources, energy, commitment, and focus, but the results and the Master's reward are well worth it. I'm sure that to bury our one talent might seem less work in the moment, but it's disastrous in the long run. You have to keep taking Holy Spirit-inspired action and measure the success of each step by evaluating if the goals that you set for that step were accomplished. We are called to faithfully steward the treasures of King Jesus. Let's not tire being fruitful.

Our Real life dream of thriving multiple cities will involve equipping multiple church planters to start marketplace churches in multiple U.S. locations and across the globe. This is a lofty vision. Many of us will be overwhelmed by the magnitude of a vision that either hasn't taken its first breath, or is in its infancy stage. The key to success, without letting our heads spin, is to envision steps appropriate to our maturity stage. When going after your endeavor, don't compare your beginning with someone else's middle or end.

For example, we desire to involve all of our 3Bs—bodies, buildings, and bucks—to grow the entrepreneurs in our city but, for now, our capacity only allows us to support them with two of the 3 Bs. With the first B— bodies— Real Life personnel and volunteers are leading entrepreneurial programs, workshops, trainings, and networking events. With the second B—buildings—we are offering private offices and common co-working space. We haven't built enough capacity for our third B—bucks—to have investment capital for entrepreneurial startups. We are learning to be patient and pace our compassion to match our capacity and find joy even in the limitations we experience as we expand the kingdom of God in our city among the entrepreneurs we serve.

It is important to remember envisioning the future is only as good as your desire to take divinely-inspired action toward that future. Leaders must sometimes be willing to become unpopular until their model is proven, boldly taking risks as they put structures and systems in place to ensure the success of their venture.

Why do we need to measure? We need to know if the church is doing its job. One day the Master will measure His ROI (return on investment) (Matt. 25). We had better measure along the way to assure we are found faithful.

How do we measure it? We are convinced we must measure, but how will we measure the church's success? Do we measure in numbers or some intangibles that are hard to define? Are numbers good, constricting, or bad? There is nothing inherently bad in numbers, neither when it comes to people, money, or buildings. The critical point is what we measure.

Admittedly, there is a difference between measuring quantity versus quality. Quality means different things to different people. It's sometimes hard, but it's possible to measure both. If you are measuring spiritual maturity it helps if the pastors establish a baseline for what they consider a disciple to be and then measure those characteristics as evident in the lives of the congregants. For example, we can measure conversions, water baptisms, the number of people becoming whole-life disciples, and those brought off drugs. We can also measure economic impact by counting the number of entrepreneurs helped to start a new business or academic scholarships for business education.

Measuring kids brought off the street or helped to improve in school, those sent to an entrepreneurial program, or teens given scholarships for summer camp shows the way the church impacts the life of the next generation. Although it's hard to measure social capital, we can still measure the community projects the church gets involved in or the civic organizations it engages and the relationships the congregants establish with people from the community. We can measure homeless people housed, or unemployed people trained for jobs. Whatever your church is focused on, you can measure the impact you are making in your community and on the marketplace. The numbers you count give you an opportunity to celebrate the way your church grows and supports your community and advances the Kingdom of God.

Bodies. Churches for Monday count the people they reach in the Sunday-to-Monday Bridge, not only the Sunday worship event. We can count the unemployed we train for work, the entrepreneurs we convene for a meetup, the singles gathering at our facility for coffee, the kids' playdates our daycares offer to the community. There are many opportunities to impact people in the marketplace and we can measure the lives we touch by counting bodies.

Bucks. Churches for Monday count the budget of the church, but also the economic development they cause for the local economy and beyond, and the upward economic lift they facilitate for the congregants and people from the community. Churches can help develop or scale business by training the business owners or investing in the business. They can add to the workforce by providing job training or job-retraining and add economic value by supporting young people with academic or training scholarships.

Buildings. Buildings are great assets to the church and can become a valuable asset to the community. Churches for Monday count how many ways the buildings are used to create touches with the community and provide vital, meaningful resources to further the education, work, and play. For example, empty Sunday school classrooms can be used to house entrepreneurs looking for an office space during the week. The fellowship halls can be rented out for community events, birthday parties, bridal showers, or business trainings. The gymnasiums can bring for sports the youth of the community who may otherwise never come to church on Sunday. The church yards can be used for photography sessions by budding photographers or moms with kids for play-dates. Having people experience your facility outside of Sunday makes it likely they may visit your church in the future.

We can label the 3 Bs as passé, not spiritual enough, and throw them away. Still we cannot escape the fact that any earthly enterprise operates on bodies, budgets, and buildings (or virtual spaces).

We can pretend we are not going to count the 3 Bs—but we all know we will. We have to. Otherwise, one Sunday we might be meeting on the sidewalk because someone did not account for the right budget. The pressing question is not, do we discard the scorecard, but "Can we thoughtfully revamp it for greater Kingdom impact, which counts both the Sunday worship and the Monday mission?"

A Movement

Churches preparing for Monday are on the rise and are becoming a movement. They equip whole-life disciples on Sunday for mission at work on Monday. They guide believers on how to effectively translate the gospel for their postmodern friends to hear. If you are someone who has not engaged the 8-to-5 window for impact, but are curious about it, this is an invitation to re-enter the mission of God with renewed fervor to see you and others transform.

A Real-Life Story of a Church for Monday Engaged in Mission Outside of Its Church Walls

Rose City Church in Pasadena, California, has awakened to the fact Christian neighborly love has an economic aspect and has begun to love its neighbors into financial stability. At Rose City, the body of believers is sent out of their church doors with creativity and hospitality. They are committed to building partnerships that spread God's love in their community throughout the week, but it is not just the "scattered church," which brings economic shalom to their city. The body of Christ at Rose City has found that discipleship is a holistic experience that forms their community into a group of people ready to put their spirituality into practice in the marketplace through a common endeavor. Here is Rose City Church's story shared with me by Pastor Dan Davidson in a written interview.

When Pastor Dan Davidson re-opened Rose City in 2009, he became concerned about the group of homeless youth who camped out on the church's grounds. With one of the largest community colleges in Southern California just a block away, he was not surprised to find homeless youth sleeping in the church parking lot. He began to engage the teens by offering food and clothes, but this increased the number of youth coming—and that upset the neighbors. Realizing he had to help in a better way and that there was a gap in supportive services, Pastor Davidson found an old coffee cart on the church property and began training the youth to get jobs in the area's growing gourmet coffee industry. They lovingly named this coffee cart Rosebud."

Rosebud traveled around LA, empowering homeless and transitional-aged youth as they practiced their newfound craft—serving an amazing cup of coffee. Rosebud's work has led the church to establish a permanent cafe in Pasadena, which they named after their little cart. Today, the body of believers continues to persist in their mission of crafting coffee, community, and cause. Pastor Davidson says:

> Our story matters deeply to the residents of Pasadena. A progressive city with more than 1,000 nonprofits, we had no trouble finding our loyal and supportive customers as the first social enterprise cafe. And though our story may draw them to the shop, it's our hospitality that keeps them coming back. Not only do we seek to be one of the best coffee shops in town, but we also, and more importantly, seek to be the most beloved coffee shop in town. It's our gift of hospitality and community served alongside a beautifully crafted latte with homemade lavender syrup that keeps our sales numbers growing.

Homeless youth are taught job skills in a caring, hands-on mentoring environment. Rosebud pairs one barista to volunteer his or her time with youth, anyone from eighteen to twenty-five, who then trains at the brick-and-mortar location for four-to-six months. Through the training, Rosebud works with its partner nonprofits to help find housing units to keep the young employees off the streets and to identify additional vocational training opportunities.

The youth-trainees take special pride in learning the flavor profile of the different coffee beans and crafting a delicious cup of java. It is often something profound that happens when the transitional-aged youth make their first cup of coffee for a client who then pays and thanks them for their services. It is as though a rebirth of their human dignity ensues. These young people often have been given necessities for living, because they have lacked fundamental resources, but they have never been asked to contribute. The moment they are recognized as bona fide creators and contributors of value in the marketplace, something within them is unleashed. They can see themselves as givers instead of takers, as producers of goods and services that others appreciate, and that helps them dream of a hopeful future. Pastor Davidson sums it up well: "These youth have been given many hand-me-downs, but that only have exacerbated their low self-esteem. When they were asked to contribute at the Rosebud Café by creating specialty coffees, using their training to recognize complex coffee flavors that is when they have come alive. They take pride in being able to work and contribute value to society."

This real-life story of a Church for Monday that bridges the sacred/secular divide in the marketplace offers much by way of inspiration and instruction. Asking the transitional-aged youth to work and create value in the local economy honors both their human dignity and their creative streak, which bears the image of Creator God. There is nothing more empowering to a person than to be given the opportunity to create cultural goods and services, and to shape the economy by doing honest work.

Recovering Relevance: Practitioners and Thought Leaders on Being a Church for Monday

A Marketplace Vision

When I first got a vision of the church in the middle of the marketplace, I thought, "Am I completely alone in this line of thinking?" I could picture it, but had not yet processed a theology for it, so I had a hard time explaining, even to my husband, what a church in the marketplace looks like. God has worked much in my own understanding and connected me with many who have seen a similar reality for the church of the twenty-first century.

Since then I have been a part of faith-integration think tanks, formed friendships with people who have felt the church-and-marketplace disconnect, and have worked toward closing the Sunday-to-Monday gap. They are thought-leaders and practitioners who deal with the reductionism of the gospel in their daily vocations. I have asked some of them to re-envision for us what the church could look like if it equips believers on Sunday for mission at work on Monday. You can read more about the contributors in the end notes. I asked this question: "Based on the current trends of declining church attendance and the faith-and-marketplace integration gap, what are some ways for the church to reestablish credibility in the marketplace?" Let's see a few examples of how to do that well in different sectors of society.

Religion: How Can the Church Re-envision Its Place in Society?

Tom Nelson leads Made to Flourish, [1] a network that empowers pastors and their churches to integrate faith, work, and economic wisdom for the flourishing of their communities. As one of the City Network Leaders of Made to Flourish, I have attended many think-tank sessions and heard Tom's heart as we wrestled together with how to close the Sunday-to-Monday gap and be biblically faithful, theologically informed, and missionally aligned with the call of God for His church. We have dreamed together of how the church can reclaim its place in the public arena, equip believers to share holistic faith at work, and regain credibility. In all of our conversations, Tom has encouraged us that the bride of Christ will finish strong, and the church has always been God's Plan A to take the gospel message to the world. Tom's love for the church is contagious and inspiring. In his book, *The Economics of Neighborly Love*, he gives thoughtful answers about the role of the church in the marketplace.

> I believe the wind of the Spirit is blowing across our nation and the globe, stirring up churches and church leaders to strategically address the Sunday-to-Monday gap, to more passionately and intentionally bring faith, work, and economics together in a seamless fabric of missional faithfulness and fruitfulness. In a time when the Christian church is increasingly perceived as adding little value to a community, doors for local church gospel mission are opening wide as a result of faithful and thoughtful church engagement of work and economics.
>
> In his book *The Coming Jobs War*, Jim Clifton, chairman and CEO of the Gallup Association, summarizes conclusions from data gathered by surveying over 120,000 people in 150 countries of the world. Clifton writes, "Six years into our global collection effort, we may have already found

the single most searing, clarifying, helpful, world-altering fact. What the whole world wants is a good job." [2] What will the church's response be to this cry in this moment in history? While the world is crying out for jobs and for greater economic opportunity, churches are beginning to respond in very encouraging ways. Local church leaders are building into their strategic planning not only growing evangelism, attendance, and small group discipleship goals, but also job creation and wealth creation targets.

All too often, businesspeople in the church are seen primarily as candidates for serving on the building or finance committees. While these are good places to serve, what if these gifted servants of God were released to put more of their energy into what they do best—creating jobs and building economic capacity in our local and global economies? What if, as a part of our local church strategies, we would seek to stoke the fires of entrepreneurship and set targets for a specific number of good jobs created each year? I would like to see us celebrate not only the missionaries we send around the globe, but also the jobs we create around the world. Let's celebrate with the same enthusiasm the formation of new for-profit businesses as we do the formation of new nonprofit organizations. What if the church we have been called to serve would invest more resources in creating sustainable, tax-generating, and charity donating jobs? How would this initiative ignite the imagination and passions of the business domain within the church?

Local churches and church leaders are not only seeking ways to build capacity, they are also increasingly mapping out their present capacity to extend neighborly love to their communities. It is crucial to see the local church not only as a dynamic organism but also as stable, well-managed institution that maintains a faithful presence in a community over the long haul.

No matter the size of the local church, it is a vital economic actor within a community. The local church often has a sizeable real estate footprint, multiple buildings, and a sizeable asset balance sheet. In many cases, a growing local church is a job creator and significant employer with the opportunity to create environments where employees flourish. The local church can set the bar for leadership and management excellence, both in the profit and non-profit sectors.

What does a more intentional faith, work, and economics focus look like in a local church? The answer is as varied as the theological contours of the congregation as well as the contexts in which God has sovereignly placed each local church to serve.

An increasing number of churches are thinking creatively and strategically about how to better embrace a neighborly love of compassion and capacity. High Point Church of Christ in Princeton, Texas, offers seed capital for new businesses launched by church members. Olivet Baptist Church in Chattanooga, Tennessee, underwrites college scholarships for under-resourced youth who will be the first in their families to seek a college education. Tabernacle Community Church in Grand Rapids, Michigan, sponsors the Youth Entrepreneur Leadership Program. In this program middle school students are exposed to entrepreneurship teaching for seven weeks during the summer. Students develop business plans and present them to local entrepreneurs in a "Shark Tank" environment. City Hope Church in Akron, Ohio, is a new startup church, committed to strong faith, work, and economic integration. As a young church plant, City Hope Church has launched an open-choice food pantry. As the description implies, people have choice in the groceries they select at the food pantry. Those who shop and those who help the shoppers share a meal together.

When it comes to faith work and economics integration, how are you and your church doing? Are you thoughtfully addressing the Sunday-to-Monday gap? [3]

How Can Church Startups Help in Closing the Marketplace Gap?

For the past 35 years, Steve Pike has either been in the process of personally starting a new church or leading an organization that assists leaders who are in the process of starting a new church. He is the President and Founder of Urban Islands Project, an organization dedicated to increasing the presence of the church in the urban core of America's largest urban centers. Prior to Urban Islands, Steve served as the Founding Director of the Church Multiplication Network (CMN)—an organization that has assisted with the starting of over 3000 new congregations in every region of the US.

CMN is where I met Steve. My husband and I walked into his office to share our unique vision of church as a spiritual and economic engine in the community, not sure if our vision for church would fit the CMN church planters community. To our surprise, after hearing our vision, Steve shook our hands and welcomed us to CMN, then proceeded to show us the business magazines he was reading to expand his strategic thinking on how to start churches that are economically viable and spiritually impactful both to the churched and the unchurched. Since that day, Steve has been a valuable friend and a wise guide who has cheered my husband and me to the successful start of Real Life Church. My team and I were blessed with many mentors on our church planting journey, but Steve is one of the most insightful individuals I know when it comes to church startups that close the church-to-marketplace gap. Shares Steve:

> Part of the reason I've been so focused on starting new churches is because of the trend of declining church attendance. Years ago, I took seriously the concept the definition of insanity is to keep doing the same thing over and over and hoping for different results. Preferring sanity over insanity, I asked the question, "What does the church need to do differently to reverse the declining church attendance trend?" The answer to that question led me to become involved in starting new faith communities that were willing to forego tradition in favor of faithfully incarnating the Gospel using contextually appropriate methods and models.

In order for this approach to be effective, I realized we needed to replace the question, "How do we start another church?" With a question, "How do we make disciples in this cultural context?" The first question focuses on the institution of the church. The second question focuses on the mission of Jesus out of which the church will emerge. Deciding to let form follow function resulted in a new freedom for the form of the local church to be appropriately informed by the context in which the disciple-making community was emerging. The result was a diversity of forms of churches that are allowing the presence of the church to seep into the corners of society where its presence had been missing or rare.

One of those "corners" where the presence of the Church has been rare at best has been the marketplace. The relationship of the church to marketplace leaders has previously been primarily transactional. The unspoken message to marketplace leaders has been, "You go make money and give it to us so we can use it for ministry. In exchange, we will provide a spiritual haven so you can wash the dirt of doing business off your soul." No wonder the presence of the church has been rare in the marketplace.

However, over the past several decades, as form has been allowed to follow function, the relationship of the church to the marketplace has started to move in a promising direction. Ministry leaders have shifted their view of marketplace leaders from seeing them only as cash cows to be milked to seeing them as anointed colleagues called by Jesus to be with Him on mission. The result is the church is beginning to reestablish her credibility in the marketplace. Here are some ways I am observing this happening.

1. Increasingly, the church views marketplace leaders as sent ones whose endeavors on Mondays are just as holy as the Sunday worship gatherings. Discipleship processes are shifting from "preparing you to serve in a church ministry"

to "preparing you to act effectively as a disciple of Jesus in the marketplace."

2. Starting new churches in urban neighborhoods has been inhibited by the funding model that assumes all the operating income of a church must come from tithes and offerings alone. This is problematic because urban meeting spaces tend to be smaller and cost more resulting in an unsustainable financial reality of lower income and higher costs. An emerging wave of urban church starters is funding their endeavors with a variety of funding streams that include healthy partnerships with marketplace leaders.

3. Increasingly, urban church starters are utilizing a "diversified portfolio" of revenue streams as opposed to the conventional tithes and offerings only model. The diversified revenue streams tend to fall into 5 categories.

• Tithes and offerings (this will always be part of the funding plan for a church)

• Donor based funding (contributions received from people outside the missional reach of the church)

• Co-vocational (revenue received through work done by the church starter), non-profit partnerships (revenue or cost savings produced through partnership with compatible non-profit organizations in the target community), for-profit partnerships (revenue produced via the production of for-profit goods and services).

4. Jettisoning tradition based church forms in favor of forms built on mission has led to all manner of creative blends of faith communities in partnership with for-profit businesses.

• Coffee shop churches (for profit coffee shop during the week, gathering place for the church on weekends)

• Dance churches (dance studio during the week, gathering place for the church on the weekends)

• Young professional team churches (a group of young, employed professionals deliberately move into a neighborhood to be the catalyst for a new neighborhood focused faith community), etc.

5. The idea the church starter (or lead pastor) has to be the catalyst of everything is quickly becoming a relic from the past. An increasing number of church starters are recruiting team members to assist them with generating revenue. For example, since, church starters have to be effective at recruiting people to the cause, they can use their recruiting gifts to invite an entrepreneur to become part of the church team and begin a complementary church and business simultaneously. This overcomes the problem of pastors who lack business skills and vice versa. These startups generally take longer to get off the launchpad, but also tend to be much more financially stable for the long haul.[4]

I'm convinced that overcoming the faith-and-marketplace integration gap will lead to a significant expansion of the presence of the church in the neediest sectors of our society. Successfully overcoming this challenge will be especially impactful in urban communities, which tend to have a disproportionate impact on the trajectory of popular culture. Faith and marketplace leaders, working in alignment, can be used by God to change the destiny of cities and nations.

Government: How Can the Church Re-envision Its Role in Government?

Virginia State Senator Amanda Chase moved with her family from Sheffield, Alabama, to Virginia when she was eleven years old. Chase was among the majority of believers who did not involve themselves in politics. I interviewed her, and here's what she said. "I remember I was sitting in church with my husband and four children, and I felt God speak to my heart in a way He never had before. I knew when I left service that day, God wanted me to run for the senate state seat in the year 2015. I was not political at all. I voted on Election Day and that was it, but I could not deny the call God gave me."

Chase believes government and politics can play a pivotal role in God's work of reconciliation. Unfortunately, the church tends to avoid politics in order to avoid controversy, instead of educating themselves on issues and candidates. There is a great disadvantage for the church to not engage in the political world because the vote of the people makes a difference for the state of the country. Says Chase, "I volunteered with the Family Foundation, a non-partisan group that encourages people to register to vote and educate themselves by producing a scorecard so people know what the candidates stood for. I had churches refuse to put those in their foyers because they associated voting with government and politics."

In a democracy, the people have the right to decide who goes into leadership. This gives believers an opportunity to influence the public arena with biblical core values by electing leaders that exemplify such beliefs. "The church is missing an opportunity," Chase says, "by not researching and comparing the values of candidates running for office with the values of the Word of God. We can't leave our faith at the church door. We have to understand the Holy Spirit is with us 24/7. For people to divide their spiritual lives and the rest of their lives is very misinformed. God saved us so we can serve Him in what we are doing. Why would we not embrace the political sector, too, since it significantly affects our culture?" Chase reminds us that America was founded on biblical principles, and it is up to the American believers to continue those values going forward.

Chase encourages believers to pray for our political arena and find creative ways to encourage our legislators. She has one pastor who partners with he in prayer and encouragement for her and her family. That partnership has lifted the spirits of both Chase and her husband as they have continued in politics. She encourages the church to reach out to their political leaders, embrace them, and give support as they run after the calling God has given them. Chase says, "I tell my staff every day, 'we may be in a Senate's office, but this is a ministry.' We have hurting people reaching out to us in need of help and service. I joke with my staff that we are the hands and feet of Jesus, but we are also lepers who no one wants to associate with, because there are two things not to be mentioned: religion and politics." She is adamant this is a myth that must be torn down.

Both topics of Christian faith and politics are vital and are great points of discussion because they make a generational and eternal difference. The church must wake up and become educated about the importance of understanding and supporting politicians who affect the systemic life in our country. In order to follow Senator Chase's advice to stop separating politics and faith, the church needs to recognize God has called His people to be a blessing in all spheres of life, including the political arena, so they may re-establish His values of justice, mercy, and provision for all. [5]

Business: How Can the Church Re-envision Its Role in Business?

To some in the Christian community, "business" is a dirty word, connoting themes of unbridled greed and ethical compromise. While it is true the worldly temptations of the private sector are ever present and can certainly bring out the worst in people, business also provides some of the most redemptive spiritual opportunities. I asked my good friend and business owner, Chuck Proudfit, who leads thousands of Christians to impact the workplace in Cincinnati, Ohio to give us some insights from his daily work.

> My 'tent making' takes the form of business consulting. As the founder and president of SKILLSOURCE, I lead a practice that develops strong leadership, healthy culture, and winning strategy for our clients. As a working Christian, consulting becomes a powerful platform for me to bring the light of Christ to the darkest corners of the marketplace. The private sector is a complicated, fast-paced venue filled with disruptive change and intractable challenges. It is the wisdom of God's Word, and the inspiration of the Holy Spirit that gives Christians superior solutions to business problems. Every time I deliver excellence in a consulting project, I earn the credibility to speak about my faith.

Jesus anticipated all of this in Luke 10. As He sends out the seventy disciples to reach surrounding towns and villages and share the Good News of Christ, He provided a process for successful spiritual engagement that I have adapted to consulting. We are to go about our business and give a warm greeting to those we encounter. Where we are rebuffed, we simply move on to build relationships with those who warm to us. As we get to know them and learn of their challenges, we minister to their felt needs. When they express appreciation or inquire about us, they open the door for us to share our faith testimonies. From there, conversations can go anywhere."

I have followed this process with excellent results. As I solve client problems—my version of "ministering to the sick"—I earn the credibility to speak spiritually into their lives. Over the years, I've had dozens of faith conversations, sparked a wide range of spiritual searches, and led people to the Lord! I follow this process not just with clients, but across all the stakeholders in my consulting work, including employees, contractors, suppliers, regulators, investors, and even competitors."

Jesus' direction in Luke 10 is easily adaptable to any form of work. If every working Christian were following it, we would have a dramatic impact, very much like the Early Church. In *The Rise of Christianity*, Rodney Stark recounts how this first took place, with the Church growing from 120 believers in the Upper Room in Jerusalem to half the adult population of the Roman Empire within just 250 years.

I realize that contemporary Christianity gravitates to ministry 'projects' through the local church, where we go out en-masse for community service, or embark on mission trips that take us all over the world. My point is we can see our everyday work as our mission field and the people around us at work as those to whom we can minister.

To the everyday working Christian, the local church can be a catalyst for this type of faith integration at work. Anything that isn't sinful is sacred, so all work is worship, and secularism is a non-biblical concept. When pastors preach this foundation on Sunday from the stage and then celebrate the spiritual impact of working Christians on stage, it affirms—it can literally launch—working Christians to become faith active at work.

Even more powerful is the local church pastor who visits congregants' workplaces to learn about their weekday lives, offer spiritual encouragement, and share spiritual insights. "When Christians see business as our vocation and work as worship, then we become a transformational force for spiritual change throughout the marketplace. If one Christian can contribute to spiritual flourishing in a narrow segment of business, can we imagine the flourishing that all of us can bring together to our communities, and to our nations, where we work and where we live?[6]

Technology: How Can the Church Re-envision Its Role in Technology?

Today's technology evolves at a break-neck pace. Many church leaders have mixed thoughts about technological innovation. Few pastors know how to leverage technology to connect with young people who use it. Some even fear this idea. Leah Archibald is a veteran of the high tech industry and sold IT systems integration software before joining the Theology of Work Project. She believes technology can play a pivotal role in God's work of reconciliation. Furthermore, she argues church leaders who leverage technology will be rewarded with deeper connections and bigger impact among the people they serve.

In my first professional job, I worked for a digital marketing agency. I ran online teaching events called 'webinars' that sold chief technology officers on the benefits of IT integration software. On the surface, there was nothing spiritual about 'enterprise resource planning.' It was just a job, I thought, and I often resented my work had no value in God's Kingdom.

Looking back now, after spending almost as much time writing about the Bible as I did hawking ERP software, I can see the fingerprints of God all over this technology. The software helped people get just the right amount of materials they needed to do their jobs—not too much, not too little, and at exactly the right time. That helped them fulfill God's original intention for human work and for creation. God put people in charge of creation in Genesis 1:26, and in Genesis 2:16–17. He instructed them to obey limits in what they take. Good enterprise resource planning helps people do just that. My work marketing ERP software was a small contribution to restoring the world to God's created order.

In many different areas of life, technology helps people redeem what's broken in the world and do the work God created them to do. And technology can be a great way to connect with people in simple, economic, and unobtrusive ways. But there are fears about technology, too, especially within the church. Wise Christians have known for centuries that it's important to slow down to connect with God and with other people. With the omnipresence of technology, we're tempted to check our smartphones every waking moment for the next hit of information. Online social media connects us with people around the globe, but too often at the expense of connections with our neighbors or families right in front of us.

Isaiah 43:5–6 says, "I will gather you and your children from east and west. I will say to the north and south, 'Bring my sons and daughters back to Israel from the distant corners of the earth.'" Technology such as satellite telephony, international texting networks, and even emoji programming can be part of God's redemptive work of bringing people together.

The challenge for churches is that many pastors are not technology strategists. They're trained in teaching, pastoring, and leading a congregation. Mastering new technology can seem like a frustrating distraction. For this reason, churches should team up with savvy technologists who can help them use these mediums to reach people. Large churches may have a digital marketing person on staff. For churches that don't have that luxury, parachurch ministries can help. CV North America uses social media and marketing technology to connect people to local churches. www.Butler.Church provides social graphics and content for churches that do not have a paid staff member to do so.

Christians are increasingly looking to technology to help them grow spiritually and to connect their faith to their work. The Theology of Work Project, my current employer, helps two million Christians a year apply the Bible to their daily work. Google search is a big driver to theologyofwork.org. This shows that Christians are hungry for help with their work, and they're going online to find answers.

The church can meet people where they are by learning about today's technologies and how they connect us. It starts with discerning the positives and negatives in each technology and pursuing how we can use it to further God's redemptive work in the world. [7]

Women and Millennials: How Can the Church Re-envision the Way It Makes Room for Women and Millennials?

Many church leaders are not sure how to navigate their relationships with millennials as they see a growing disconnect between the church and the young people in our culture. They feel the tension of the age gap and often are tempted to give up trying to connect. In addition, another gap, not a new one, but newly highlighted, adds to the tensions in the church: the gender gap. But if the church will equip its congregants to bridge the Sunday worship to Monday work gap, then the church cannot continue to sidestep the church to Women, or the church to millennials gaps.

Monday faith that practices whole life discipleship in all spheres of life involves the whole person of both genders, male and female, and in all stages of life from young to old. I asked Karley Hatter, a twenty-four-year-old millennial and recent seminary graduate, who aims to build strategic relationships in the faith, work, and economic integration networks, to re-envision how the church can make room for women and millennials.

> August 2017, just weeks before I embarked on my journey to Fuller Theological Seminary in Los Angeles, my pastor asked me, "Why would you go to seminary?" As my mind started to spin, the only question that came to my mind was, "Why wouldn't I?" Ever since I became a Christian, I was captivated by the desire to preach. All through college, I found myself leading Bible studies, preaching, and teaching. Going to seminary was something I never thought would be questioned; it was always something I thought was incredibly clear. As I continued to see my male colleagues encouraged to attend seminary, my pastor's questioning continued to plague my spirit. "I had been attending this church for years, and this congregation had been instrumental in shaping my theology. However, my pastor's question led to more questions about my call. *Where was my seat at the table? Where are the women?* As a millennial woman who has dreams of preaching in a pulpit, exploring my giftings in ministry, becoming an entrepreneur, charting new territory, this question was disorienting. The lack of encouragement and support to attend seminary during this season shaped my ecclesiology and theology of vocation."
>
> Over time, I have become grateful for my pastor's question. It provoked in me an earnest desire to deconstruct and reconstruct my ecclesiology and devote an entire season to letting the Spirit of God reshape my theology. What would I reimagine the church to look like? Feel like? Sound like? My seminary journey has been layered with complexities, frustrations, and joys. Seminary has deeply equipped me for the spiritual journey that lies

ahead, but most of all has helped me see the expansive nature of God.

I would reimagine a church that fully affirms the roles of women in leadership and ministry—where both male and female are equally championed. The church at large has failed to spiritually equip women, as well as younger people's minds and voices. One of the biggest questions young people are asking today is, "What am I called to do?" The church has often failed to help young people vocationally discern their work, leaving them in spaces of spiritual immaturity.

If the church continues to fail to ask young people the right questions around faith, work, and calling, their sense of community and belonging will remain detached from the church. I deeply desire that the church would reimagine what it would look like to focus on the *whole self*. Miroslav Volf described the vision of a whole-life-discipleship church well: "We need to build and strengthen mature communities of vision and character who celebrate faith as a way of life as they gather before God for worship and who, sent by God, live it out as they scatter to pursue various tasks in the world."

Steven Argue from the Fuller Youth Institute talks about helping our young adults go from faith to 'faith-ing.' He says that "programming also buys into these pre-conceived notions where more emphasis is placed on getting people 'in' or counting conversions, never realizing that these same people leave the church because, in their own words, they've 'outgrown it.' One-time conversions or the length of being a Christian don't necessarily speak to spiritual maturity." Cultivating space for young people to fully mature in their personhood while engaging in questions of vocation have the ability to equip the next generation to make catalytic shifts within the church. The church has a unique opportunity to embrace younger generations who are searching for a place to belong, specifically in wrestling with conversations around faith and vocation.

Young people like me want to show up in church and celebrate our vocations, work, and passions as acts of faith. I imagine creatives, artists, entrepreneurs, women, men, all races and ethnicities and ages representing the modern-day church. [8]

Gen Z: How Can the Church Re-envision Discipling the Gen Z?

It might go without saying, but today's teenagers are not growing up in their grandparents' or their parents' world—not even in their twenty-something cousin's world. Rapid changes in technology, communication, science, law, and worldview are creating a world for teenagers that leaves many parents, church leaders, and other mentors feeling perplexed. I asked David Kinnaman and the Barna Group who have been studying the Gen Z's culture, motivations, and beliefs to help us re-envision how the church can disciple the youngest generation.

Of course, changes to culture are not changes to the essence of what it means to be human. Teens today, like teens of long ago, wrestle with insecurity, bullying, boredom, loneliness, raging hormones, and paralyzing doubt. They navigate their first crushes, question their parents' beliefs, and dream of their future. Perhaps what adults need first and foremost to remind ourselves is this: We were there once too. They are not so very different from us at that age.

"Yet it is foolish to believe teens—even Christian teens— are immune to the surrounding culture. Barna analysts find evidence of a creeping lack of purpose and meaning that comes sharply into focus when we look at what Gen Z teens say they want to accomplish before age thirty. Barna offered the same list of options to millennials in 2013; here are both generations' answers presented side by side, for comparison.

I Want to Accomplish ━━━━━━ Before Age 30

Gen Z		Rank		Millennials
Finish my education	66%	1	59%	Become financially independent
Start a career	66%	2	52%	Finish my education
Become financially independent	65%	3	51%	Start a career
Follow my dreams	55%	4	40%	Find out who you really are
Enjoy life before you have the responsibilities of being an adult	38%	5	31%	Follow my dreams
Find out who you really are	31%	6	29%	Become more mature spiritually
Travel to other countries	21%	7	28%	Get married
Get married	20%	8	24%	Enjoy life before you have the responsibilities of being an adult
Become more mature spiritually	16%	9	21%	Become a parent
Become a parent	12%	10	20%	Travel to other countries
Care for the poor and needy	9%	11	9%	Care for the poor and needy
Try to become famous or influential	9%	12	5%	Try to become famous or influential

U.S. teens ages 13–18, n=1,490, Nov. 4–16, 2016. U.S. adults 18–29, n=1,000, June 25–July 1, 2013.

The trends Barna identified among millennials—high priority on career achievement, low priority on personal and relational growth—are amplified in Gen Z. Fewer teens are interested in starting a family or becoming more spiritually mature. Nearly two out of five want to spend their twenties enjoying life before they have the responsibilities of being adult—significantly higher than the one-quarter of millennials who said this.

More than half of teens want to follow their dreams, yet just three in ten want to find out who they really are. But the faith segmentation on these statements is interesting. Teens with no religious affiliation are much more likely than engaged Christians to want both to follow their dreams (62 percent vs. 42 percent) and to find out who they really are (41 percent vs. 25 percent). This may indicate an impulse in those with no faith to seek greater meaning.

Engaged Christians, as we might expect, are more likely to say spiritual maturity is a goal (46 percent) and a bit more likely to say they'd like to get married (29 percent) and have children (16 percent) before age thirty. Yet these low percentages suggest the cultural tide against marriage—or at least toward delaying it—is tugging at faithful Christians along with everyone else. Perhaps many teens consider marriage and parenting to be "adult responsibilities" that they are planning to avoid during their twenties.

The Primary Mark of Adulthood:
Gen Z vs. Millennials   ● Gen Z   ● Millennials

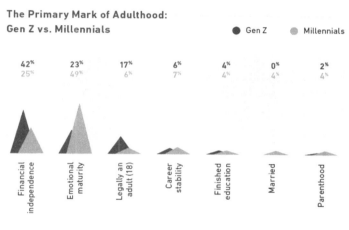

US teens ages 13–18, n=1,490, Nov. 4–16, 2016. US adults 18–29, n=563, June 25–July 1, 2013.

How will they know when they have arrived at adulthood? Barna also asked this question among millennials in 2013—and the generational differences are stark. Financial independence looms large for many teens in a way it did not for eighteen- to twenty-nine-year-old millennials; doubtless the country's (and their parents') financial problems since the Great Recession are a big influence here. Emotional maturity, on the other hand—of such supreme importance to many millennial twenty-somethings—is significant to fewer than one in four teenagers. It will be interesting to see if these priorities shift as Gen Z moves into adulthood.

There is, of course, nothing inherently wrong with having enough money to care for family and meet financial obligations. But the New Testament writers are clear that making pursuit of wealth one's primary life goal is spiritually dangerous and even destructive. Gen Z is certainly not alone in their battle to put wealth in its proper place—this is an arena where American Christianity overall has struggled to maintain its prophetic witness to a culture consumed with consuming. Perhaps walking alongside the next generation will also help older Christians rethink our own relationships with material success and personal happiness.

How can Gen Z become disciples in a post-Christian culture? Thankfully, the church has centuries of experience communicating the gospel across religious, linguistic and cultural divides. We call it "missions." When a missionary immerses herself in a culture different from her own, she doesn't expect the people who live there to speak and act and think like people from home—in fact, she expects quite the opposite: that she will have to change in order to connect with people.

A similar situation confronts churches today. Will older Christians insist that the youngest generation must speak, act and think like us? Or will we help young exiles become and remain the people of God in their own culture?

If the latter, then Gen Z disciple-making must actively engage a two-way dynamic: faith in light of culture; culture in light of faith. How we follow Christ is inevitably shaped by the culture in which we find ourselves. But it is at least equally true that the surrounding culture is transformed as we are transformed in Christ. How can we equip Gen Z not just with information about faith but also with critical thinking and experiences that deepen faith? Parents and educators, especially, are positioned to proactively guide growing teens to think well about living for Christ in a post-Christian culture.

The pace of cultural change may feel overwhelming, but don't be discouraged. Even the gates of hell cannot prevail against the church—and that promise is for God's people in Generation Z too. [9]

Media: How Can the Church Re-envision Its Role in Media?

I asked Cassandra Ferguson, a radio and television talk show host, to share how God led her to media, and about the ways God has provided for her in pursuing the call of God on her life. Cassandra encourages church leaders to no longer be a sleeping giant, but to be the voice of truth God has called them to be through media.

In today's society, media plays an important role in the influence of an individual, a family, and a community. Key decisions are made based off of what someone has seen or heard from radio, television, or on social media. With media your message gets out farther across a larger and wider audience, whether you are in China or in New York City once the information is released you will see or hear it quickly.

Because the church has a mandate from God to 'Go Ye And Teach All Nations' (Matthew 28:19), media is the vehicle that can be used to fulfill it. In an instant the gospel can be heard all over the world from a media platform."

Often church leaders do not leverage the media platform because they lack resources or fear of the unknown. I have heard some even say they 'don't want to become famous,' when in reality, that is a prideful statement camouflaged with a false sense of humility. There is a reason God wants to make your name great (Genesis 12:2).

Several years ago, God gave me a vision to pull businesswomen together to connect and share business strategies. At that time, I owned and operated a mortgage company, and my networking group Business Women On The Move was planning their first event. Friends in media offered me opportunities to promote the event. After a radio appearance, the host said to me, "Have you ever considered radio? You will do very well on the air, you have a great radio voice." I immediately thought of my inadequacy and lack of experience and said, "Who, me?" Fear stepped in and I said, "No, not at all." For years I thought about his question and my response. Feeling like it could have been a missed opportunity, I promised God that if the opportunity were to ever come again, I would walk through the door.

Ten years later it happened. During a very difficult time in Baltimore, the vision came to me as I watched news coverage of our youth in an uproar on the streets. They needed a platform of wisdom, leadership, purpose, and celebration. I sought wise counsel from someone who had been in media for years. She listened to my vision, made suggestions on which local stations to call, and said these three words to me, "Make the Call." I called several local stations and pitched my radio show vision. By the end of the day, I had gotten several invitations to do what is called 'Block Radio.'

We are now going into our fourth year in media, and God continues to give us provision. Doors and opportunities continue to open by saying yes to God and wanting to bring a solution to someone else's problem. God is using media to bring awareness of His glory to the earth. "But [the time is coming when] the earth shall be filled with the knowledge of the glory of the Lord as the waters cover the sea" (Habakkuk 2:14 NLT).

Occupying the sphere of media will not come without a fight. The enemy knows once God's church truly gains a full understanding of the level of power and influence, they will have to steward this area, it will be like a tsunami—an arrival or occurrence of something in overwhelming quantities or amounts. The church needs to occupy with power. The enemy wants to keep us in a defeated mindset. This is a key principality that operates in media. Making sure he fills God's people with fear and anxiety due to bad news.

That's when the church comes in to plant seeds of hope and truth. We proclaim God's word to shift the atmosphere. "Don't copy the behavior and customs of this world, but let God transform you into a new person by changing the way you think. Then you will learn to know God's will for you, which is good and pleasing and perfect' (Romans 12:2 NLT)."

Now the media and social media have intertwined. Both the business world and individuals are using it every day to expand their reach. They are willing to put in the time and investment. God puts it in the heart and minds of man to develop and create. As His church, we need to position ourselves for expansion and reach souls from all around the world through the waves of media. [10]

Arts and Entertainment: How Can the Church Re-envision Its Role in Arts and Entertainment?

When the church becomes a place where artists are allowed to create, the artists will produce works that will translate the glory of God to their culture. I have asked Linda Evans Shepherd, a best-selling, award-winning author, and CEO of the Advanced Writers and Speakers Association, of which I'm a member, to share from her experience how the church can re-establish its presence in the arts and entertainment space.

Consider Michelangelo, who was commissioned by Pope Julius II in the early 1500s to paint Biblical scenes on the ceiling of the Sistine Chapel. Michelangelo's paintings, like *The Creation of Adam*, were part of a series of illustrations depicting the stories of Genesis. In *The Creation of Adam*, Michelangelo illustrated the idea of God reaching out to Adam, the first man. This painting became a way for illiterate Italian peasants to 'read' the Word of God, not in print, but in brushstrokes of paint splashed across the ceiling of their own cathedral. The painting spoke to the idea that God was not only their creator but a God who reached into their lives. This was important because the people of this generation had no Bible of their own. It would be another hundred years before King James would approve the translation of the Bible into English.

Not only did artists paint messages of faith at the end of the fifteenth century, but actors also began to portray faith in morality plays such as *Everyman*, a play performed throughout the streets of England. *Everyman* was a story about good versus evil, complete with allegorical characters such as Everyman, Fellowship, (material) Goods, and Knowledge. Its message pointed to the church's belief that 'everyman' might obtain salvation through his own good deeds. While the theology of the play misses the work and grace of Christ, it was an effective way for the Catholic Church to bring their message of morality to the people.

When I was a college student, I was privileged to meet a traveling drama troupe that landed at the Baptist Student Center at Lamar University. This troupe would perform their own version of *Everyman* in the student courtyard, depicting the salvation message of grace through the work of Christ on the cross.

The play was a hit, as crowds of college kids would gather, laugh at the antics of the actors, while receiving the salvation message. It was a thrilling experience for me, as a Fine Arts major, to behold. I started my own arts ministry journey by working with the teens at my own church, where we created a traveling puppet show which we used in Vacation Bible Schools and performed to groups around town.

A few years later, I realized God was calling me to go deeper into the arts, as he called me to write the first of many Christian books, including *The Potluck Club* (a novel series) and *When You Don't Know What to Pray*. I was delighted to find the medium of publishing in which to share my faith. Today, the Christian publishing industry has come a long way, with over fifty million copies of Christian books sold annually. Despite bookstore closings, I am not worried that Christian publishing is a diminishing art form, as Ecclesiastes 12:12 states, "There is no end to the writing of many books' (NLT)."

Just as Michelangelo used the medium of paint to reach his community, and fifteenth-century thespians used the medium of drama to spread their salvation message to villagers, and modern Christians have used the medium of print to reach the church, I think it's time for the church to use the medium of the arts through the marketplace to reach the world. This brings us to the doors of Hollywood. While many believers scoff at the immorality and heathenism associated with Hollywood, there is a growing tribe of Hollywood Christians. Many of these Christians are on their own missionary journey, fighting their own battles. One show-runner, with tears in his eyes, told me that he had hoped to make a greater difference by bringing Christian characters to sitcoms and dramas. He felt he had only slowed or stopped the level of immorality that aired if he hadn't worked on the show he wrote for. He told me, "Christians aren't praying for us. They mock us, not understanding that people like me are on the front lines, really trying to make a difference.

"Not only should we be praying for people like my friend, but we should be sending even more of our young (and old) people into Hollywood. We cannot abandon this mission field if we want to reach the world. Today Hollywood has found a revival in the success of many Christian films. And Christian production companies and streaming services such as Pure Flix are working full time to create films with a message of hope. The Kendrick brothers have helped to lead this change with movies they began to produce out of their own church, Sherwood Baptist, in Albany, Georgia, starting with *Facing the Giants* (2006).

Christian movies are making a comeback since the great movies of faith, like Cecil B. DeMille's 1957 movie, *The Ten Commandments*, have aired on the silver screen. Still, we have a way to go. First, we need to pray for Christians in Hollywood. Second, we need to financially support the producers who are trying to create movies with budgets of only a couple of million dollars, compared to the multi-million dollar movies of established Hollywood. Third, we need to send Christians into work in Hollywood and to take classes and programs such as Dr. Ted Beahr's MovieGuide and Act One Program's screenwriting and producing classes. Christian films are already making a difference, and this difference will continue as Christians lend their prayers, support, talent, and young people. This is a sphere in the marketplace that we, in the body of Christ, can once again influence. [11]

Education: How Can the Church Re-envision Its Role in Education?

Education is a vast and various enterprise. We have public education and private education. Then there's preschool, elementary school, secondary school, college, and beyond. Education happens in a wide range of schools, institutions, workplaces, studios, community centers, and places of worship. Education happens within families, whether through the ordinary interactions of family life or intentional homeschooling. More than ever before in history, education takes place technologically as people learn through the Internet and other hi-tech media. Although one cannot begin to address in detail how the church might engage these vast and various educational contexts, I have asked Mark Roberts, Executive Director of Fuller's Max De Pree Center for Leadership, to offer a few fundamental biblical commitments that should guide us as we rethink the role of the church in education.

My list is not exhaustive. Far from it! So much more can and should be considered. But I hope that what I summarize here might get us thinking in new ways about the role of the church in education.

1. We must be committed to God as sovereign over all things.

Scripture repeatedly affirms that God is 'the great King over all the earth' (Psalm 47:2).[12] God's sovereign reign includes education, whether done in God's name or not. As Abraham Kuyper put it so famously, "[T]here is not a square inch in the whole domain of our human existence over which Christ, who is Sovereign over all, does not cry: "Mine!"'[13] This means that all education, including that which happens in public schools and universities, is ultimately under God's reign. It is God's business and, therefore, also the business of God's people.

2. We must be committed to stewarding faithfully the world God has entrusted to us.

In Genesis 1, God creates the world. In the so-called Cultural Mandate (Gen. 1:28), God gives to human beings the unique responsibility of being stewards of creation. Education is an essential element of this stewardship since it enables people to bear fruit while helping the world to flourish as well.

3. We must be committed to the goodness and godliness of teaching.

Those who teach in schools are doing good work, work that honors God and contributes to his purposes. Of course, some teach poorly. But those who strive to teach with excellence, to pass on what is true, and to help students learn well in both content and character are doing godly work. Teaching itself is a good thing and not only a context for evangelism. This goodness extends also to those who support classroom teaching: principals, custodians, special needs aides, etc.

4. We must be committed to being the salt of the earth in the places where education happens.

Jesus told His followers that we are the "salt of the earth" (Matt. 5:13). We are not just the salt of our families, churches, and private worlds. Rather, we are salt in and for the world. This means we must be out in the world, in places needing the salt of God's kingdom. Surely these places include public schools, secular universities, vocational centers, parent-teacher organizations, and school boards, not to mention YouTube, Facebook, and Coursera. We mustn't abandon the institutions of this world because they are too ___.

5. We must be committed to the welfare of the place where God has put us.

To the Jews who had been sent from Judah into exile in Babylon, the Lord said, "Seek the peace and prosperity of the city to which I have carried you into exile. Pray to the LORD for it, because if it prospers, you too will prosper" (Jer. 29:7 NIV). The Hebrew behind "peace and prosperity" is *shalom*, a word often translated as "peace." But shalom is much more than the absence of war. It implies prosperity, justice, and flourishing. Though our churches may not have been literally sent from one place to another, God has placed us in a particular location, a distinctive neighborhood, city, or town, so that we might seek its 'peace and prosperity.' One of the main ways we do this is through contributing to the education of children in the place God has placed us.

6. We must be committed to justice for the poor through education.

Proverbs 29:7 states that "the righteous care about justice for the poor." God calls His people to "lose the chains of injustice" (Isa. 58:6). Through education, we break the bonds of injustice, empowering people to flourish and live into their God-given responsibility as stewards of creation.

7. We must be committed to those among us who invest their lives in education.

Not all of us will be professional educators. Some are called to be teachers, administrators, and counselors. Most are not. But because we are the body of Christ together, we will show tangible care and concern for those whose work is education. We will rejoice when they rejoice and weep when they weep. We will support them with prayer and expressions of love. We will be their advocates, helping them flourish in one of the most challenging (and often underpaid) professions.

8. We must be committed to speaking the truth in love.

Though the command in Ephesians 4:15 to speak the truth in love addresses Christians in community, it also informs the church's role in education. As followers of the one who is the Truth (John 14:6), we will seek and uphold the truth in every sector of life, including history, biology, psychology, film studies, economics, and literature. We will do this, not with arrogance, but with a posture of loving servanthood. The church will fulfill its rightful role in education when it seeks above all to love children, teachers, administrators, and neighbors. Love for the poor and oppressed will be expressed through empowering education. The church will come to love not just the people educating and being educated, but also the institutions that educate. Such love is not boosterism. Rather, it comes from Christ-like love, grounded in the truth, as the church plays its rightful role as steward of God's creation. [14]

Higher Education: How Can the Church Re-envision Its Role in Higher Education?

Higher education has always been a crucial forming ground for the next generation leaders of this country. While many universities were founded as Christian schools, the reality now is quite different. Pastors often fret about sending their young people to college because they often "lose" their faith there and walk away from church. The expansion of atheistic thought on college campuses is very real. I asked Tom Thatcher, Provost at Cincinnati Christian University, to help us re-envision the role the church may have in higher education.

At first glance, the question seems like an oxymoron. It implies, at the very least, that 'the church' and/or individual congregations ever 'envisioned' a role in higher education in the first place, when in fact the opposite has often been the case. While many leading universities were founded as schools of divinity, for the past century the relationship between the higher education community and the church has been, at best, strained. Many churches have come to characterize colleges as bastions of disbelief, while university faculty tend to view churches as purveyors of blind faith. Stories abound of young adults leaving the church youth group to quickly fall victim to professors, and a total university culture that actively discourages faith expression. At the same time, many faith-based universities struggle to keep costs affordable while working with dwindling endowments, a situation that makes the Christian college experience inaccessible to most. Knowing then that many people will attend secular colleges and that universities are typically major employers for the communities that house them, how might the church begin to (re-)envision its relationship with the higher education community?

First, define reality. It is important for the church universal, and local churches, to understand the social position of the university relative to its/their own social position, both now and particularly in the near future with the maturing of Gen Z. Regardless of our excuses, the influence of colleges will increase, and the influence of churches will decrease. Preliminary studies show that the general distaste for institutional affiliation evident among millennials will become a defining characteristic of those born since 1995. Churches must embrace the fact that the emerging generation will prefer *not* to be affiliated with *any* organization unless they have to be. This will be particularly true of organizations where 'membership' might define one's identity or imply that one must believe or think in a particular way—e.g., churches. This trend will certainly impact church membership and attendance over the next three decades in a significant way. Specifically, fewer and fewer people will associate themselves with a church, even if they self-identify as Christian. One-fourth to one-third will answer the question, 'What is your religious affiliation?' with a single word: "None."

But while affiliation with a church is always optional, Gen Z's will be forced to affiliate with universities and, later, corporations simply because they must do so to acquire skills and make money. This being the case, we should expect participation in traditional religious activities, like attendance at weekend worship to decrease, while college enrollments will continue to increase. The latter will be true of both traditional undergraduate students (aged 18–25) and also, and increasingly, of adult learners enrolled in degree completion programs (accelerated or online) and graduate programs. Put simply, churches need to understand that the social position and influence of universities will expand while the social position and influence of local churches will shrink. Like it or not, the university cannot be ignored, so the burden is on us to figure out how to co-exist.

Second, congregations that seek to engage the higher education community, both students and graduates, should seriously attempt to understand actual perceptions of the church in higher education. *Actual perceptions* here basically mean what universities, as organizations, *actually* think about the church and churches, distinct from the ways that pastors tend to think that colleges think about them. While it is true that most college faculty are not active in any faith community and that many are actively opposed to traditional Christian beliefs for intellectual reasons, it is also true that even secular universities often welcome partnerships with faith-based organizations simply because these organizations assist them in reaching their enrollment targets. Colleges can only achieve their goals by attracting and retaining students. Many colleges are therefore open to, and in fact welcome, the efforts of churches and faith-based organizations to help students feel more comfortable, more at home, and more engaged in the university community. Happy students stay in school, and colleges like organizations—including churches and campus ministries—that keep students happy. Rather than continually re-drawing the ideological battle lines between Christianity and the college classroom—an approach that has never worked and can never work—congregations should ignore them and instead consider ways to partner with universities for the mutual benefit of both organizations.

Third, once channels for dialog are open, churches should seriously consider what the word *church* does and could mean in a university context. This is ultimately a question of contextualization: determining what forms and content are essential and which can be discarded to bring the gospel to a people group, in this case, the people group of college students and graduates and university employees. Traditional college students often live on campus; both residential students and commuters are generally deeply engaged in campus life; both traditional and adult learners, the latter almost by definition, are normally balancing their studies with work and family responsibilities; for both students and employees, the rhythm of the college calendar is the rhythm of life. Churches that ignore these facts by insisting that being part of a church means participating in religious activities that take place only at certain times and only in a church building are effectively ignoring the cultural context in which they are attempting to minister. Churches that seek to engage university populations, by contrast, will consider ways to make their programming more accessible to college students and employees—taking the gospel to these individuals where they live and expressing it in ways they can understand. Further, these churches will consider ways to address their message to the real issues and concerns of individuals enrolled in, and trained by, universities. And they will be especially concerned to ensure that college graduates in their mid-twenties can find a meaningful place to learn, serve, and grow as they start their careers and families.

The Church can never win the war with the university, except by ignoring it. Rather than bemoaning how college tends to push people away from the church, churches that wish to re-engage should consider ways to adapt to the university cycle and culture. Individual congregations and faith-based organizations should particularly consider ways that they can partner with universities in service of their common interest in serving and developing people and ensuring their successful entry into the workforce. Such approaches will require a new way of thinking about the relationship between the church and the college, a way of thinking that combines the shrewdness of a serpent with the gentleness of a dove.[15]

The Holy Spirit forms missional communities to incarnate the gospel in particular places, to bear living witness to Jesus Christ. Re-envisioning the role of the church in the different public sectors of daily life gives us the opportunity to form witnessing communities in the middle of the marketplace, in order to become a sign and foretaste of God's kingdom on earth.

A Real-Life Story—Shaping the Community's Culture through Art

Nestled in the heart of the Midwest is a church that leads by example in bridging the perilous Sunday-to-Monday gap. It enters the art's sector to embrace the inspiration around them and to partner with God in co-creating strong, beautiful futures for their communities and beyond.

In 1989, Christ Community Church launched its catalytic mission in Kansas City. Christ Community, founded by Tom Nelson, Lead Pastor and President of Made to Flourish, has become one church with five locations that seeks to influence its community for Jesus Christ.

In the Kansas City's Crossroads Arts District, Christ Community's Downtown Campus is a growing congregation in a flourishing neighborhood of galleries and art studios. Desiring to participate in the vibrant life of its neighborhood, the Downtown Campus intended from its inception to exist not only as space for Sunday worship but also as a space for arts engagement throughout the week. In 2013, the Downtown Campus hosted its first art exhibition. The exhibition featured works from a private collection of a Christ Community congregant. From those humble beginnings, the Four Chapter Gallery was born.

Today, the Four Chapter Gallery hosts monthly exhibitions that draw hundreds of viewers on the first Friday of each month. The gallery also hosts regular artist dinners, workshops, community events, and outreaches. Presenting approximately eight shows each year, Four Chapter Gallery maintains an active calendar and enjoys broad support from Christ Community Church and the surrounding arts community. The gallery's efforts are led by Tyler Chernesky, the Associate Pastor of the Downtown Campus, and Leigh Ann Dull, a Christ Community congregant who also serves as the director of Transform Arts.

Through The Four Chapter Gallery Christ Community Church desires to share thoughtful art and host meaningful conversations. For that reason, the gallery is committed to art with ideas. It selects exhibitions and curates programming to engage critical cultural topics like racial bias and violence, human trafficking and misogyny, homelessness and economic opportunity. Four Chapter Gallery has been critical in the spiritual development not only of patrons who have viewed art but also in the lives of the artists themselves. Multiple artists have commented upon the fair and professional treatment they've received from the gallery. They've admitted that this kind of treatment is not what they expected from a church-run gallery. The hospitality, professionalism, and kindness they've encountered have been catalytic in their spiritual journey, with some even reengaging faith as a result of exhibiting in Four Chapter Gallery.

Christ Community congregants who worship at the Downtown Campus have repeatedly affirmed the way in which the art displayed in the gallery challenges them to expand their understanding of faithful apprenticeship to Jesus. Economically, the gallery has also been of benefit to the local economy and emerging artists, who have sold artwork during First Friday exhibitions.

From its earliest days the Four Chapter Gallery's leaders have recognized the need for church leaders to more regularly embrace the work of artists, utilizing artwork in teaching moments, and coaching congregants on how they might better appreciate, engage and respect artistic works. The commitment to art and artists has been blessed by God, and has allowed Christ Community Church and Four Chapter Gallery to become a thriving site of cultural renewal in Kansas City.

Commissioning

Friends,

I hope that reading the pages of this book stirred your zeal to integrate faith and work to experience a spiritual, social, and economic transformation, spurred your imagination toward becoming a Church for Monday, and made you determined to show your neighbor that church is not only what we do on Sunday but what we live out on Monday and throughout the week. It is now time to put aside the cup of coffee we've shared while charting the path forward so we can get ready to move toward action. To be apprentices of Jesus is to practice what we learn and even practice while we learn.

From the depths of my heart I pray that you will seek God's redemptive futures for your communities so you can have eyes to see your Jeremiahs as Jesus sees them, have hearts that break for them as Jesus' does, and have compassion that pours forth from a well that never dries. You now know that our main role is to build a Sunday-to-Monday bridge to the divine grace available to the broken people in our communities. Picture with me a human connect bridge constructed of brothers and sisters in Christ— pastors, lay people, sty-at-home moms, missionaries, retirees, students, ministry directors, marketplace leaders, all caring about their church and the places they live in— who hand in hand enter the marketplace to flow the grace and truth of Jesus through their skills, talents, and spiritual gifts for the flourishing of their neighbors.

Everyone unique in their expression.

Everyone called in their particular vocation.

Everyone irreplaceable in the way they bear witness to Jesus.

All ushering the kingdom of God wherever they work, play, and rest.

Will you lock hands with this Spirit-empowered, whole-life discipleship army to continue the Connect Bridge right into your neighborhood, bringing God's shalom to the needs you see, and becoming a restorative kingdom foretaste while it's still daylight?

"May the favor of the Lord our God rest on us; establish the work of our hands for us—yes, establish the work of our hands (Psalm 90:17)."

Afterword

Dr. Svetlana Papazov has provided a well-reasoned and practical overview in *Church for Monday* for pastors and ministry leaders interested in connecting Sunday to Monday, and more specifically establishing entrepreneurial, marketplace churches for the sake of the gospel. The topic is very close to my own heart and to my ongoing work as the founding pastor and directional leader of Mosaic Church in Little Rock, AR (www.mosaicchurch.net) as well as the co-founder and president of Mosaix Global Network (www.mosaix.info).

In an opinion piece for CNN, Mel Robbins, an expert on human behavior and motivation, wrote about people and organizations known in the business sector as disrupters. "The disrupter," she wrote, "is someone [or collectively an organization] whose entire 'brand' is . . . to turn the way we do things on its head. . . . [Disrupters] break the mold, change our thinking about the mold and then hand us the new rules for how things work." By way of example, Robbins cited companies such as Amazon, Uber, Apple, and Facebook that completely changed the game in their respective industries from the way we think about retail and online shopping to how we catch a ride, use our cell phones, and connect relationally on the Internet. Disrupters such as these, she wrote, "don't fix what's broken because they don't innovate from inside the system." Rather, they operate outside conventional wisdom turning systems upside down to effect systemic change.

With such things in mind, we should recognize that Jesus Christ, himself, was (is) a disrupter. Think about it:

- He disrupted darkness and gave us light (Gen. 1:2–3)

- He disrupted the law and gave us grace (Gal. 3:23)

- He disrupted sin and gave us salvation (Rom. 10:9)

- He disrupted death and gave us life (Rom. 6:23)

- He disrupted time and gave us eternity (John 1:1–2, 14; 3:16)

If Jesus is a disrupter (and he is), surely, he expects his bride, the Church, to be one as well. More specifically, he expects believers to walk, work, and worship him together as one in and through local churches beyond the distinctions of this world that so often and otherwise divide (John 17:20–23). To the degree that believers are willing to do so, local churches can become disruptive by advancing the common good, influencing systemic change, and redeeming entire communities along spiritual, social, and financial fronts.

But therein lies the problem.

Due to the systemic segregation of churches today and in the eyes of an increasingly diverse and cynical society, the vast majority of pastors and churches in the United States have virtually no credibility when attempting to resolve the most pressing concerns of our time: namely, matters related to race, class, culture, economics, and community. Demographic shifts have brought change to America leaving pastors unable to frame the questions, shape the narrative, or influence conversations beyond their own insulated audiences. Moreover, believers today are as painfully divided as the society in which we live … and those without Christ in our communities know it. They see it. Our churches are marginalized because of it.

The typical local church, then, is not disruptive; rather, it has been disrupted. In what should be our finest hour, collective witness has been undermined by a lack of thoughtful, proactive, and holistic engagement on matters that deeply concern the society. More often than not words are spoken too late and only after problematic situations of real or perceived injustice arise or receive widespread attention. Therefore, when we do speak our words ring hollow, inauthentic, and self-serving whether spoken from the pulpit, on social media, or in the streets. Thus, in the eyes of secular society, churches and their pastors have lost the right to speak, to lead or to offer biblical perspective in moments of sociopolitical concern, confusion and crisis.

Is this not what it means to be as noisy gongs and clanging cymbals (1 Corinthians 13:1)?

To get beyond current realities and to advance a credible witness of God's love for all people in an increasingly diverse and cynical society, local churches must take intentional steps to:

- become healthy multiethnic and economically diverse reflections of their communities,

- advance social justice by establishing affiliated non-profits,

- pursue financially sustainable for-profit business enterprises.

As with an American football team, churches will have to learn to play on three fronts simultaneously in order to compete for the minds, hearts, and souls of those without Christ in a world filled with otherwise empty promises of security and significance. The three teams can be designated spiritual, social, and financial.

- The spiritual team exists to evangelize, baptize, disciple, and multiply the Christian faith.

- The social team exists to advance compassion and justice in the community.

- The financial team exists to encourage and develop small business and generate sustainable income.

As you've read in *Church for Monday*, entrepreneurial churches are on the rise in the United States and Svetlana Papazov gives us practical steps on how your church too can become a disruptor and build needed social capital to regain relevance in the marketplace. I predict such churches will become normative in the future. My book *The Coming Revolution in Church Economics: Why Tithes and Offerings are No Longer Enough and What You Can Do About It* complements *Church for Monday* and offers ways to leverage church assets to bless the community and generate sustainable income, such as Svetlana is encouraging you to do.

I appreciate that Dr. Papazov is not only a critical thinker but also an active practitioner bringing ideas to life in her own church context. In addition, her pastoral heart desires to help others learn from her experience and to see communities flourish to the glory of God. That's why she's written this book, and I share her desires. With Dr. Papazov, I believe that the time for pastors and churches to heed our collective insight and join the movement for integrated faith is now.

Dr. Mark DeYmaz

Founding Pastor and Directional Leader, Mosaic Church, Little Rock, Arkansas and Co-Founder and President, Mosaix Global Network Author of *Building a Healthy Multi-ethnic Church; Disruption: Repurposing the Church to Redeem the Community; and The Coming Revolution in Church Economics*

Notes

Key Terms and Definitions

1. "Edward B. Tylor, *Primitive Culture: Researches and Development of Mythology, Philosophy, Religion, Art, and Custom*, 2 vols. (1903; reprint ed., Cambridge, UK: Cambridge University Press, 2010). See also Edgar H. Schein, *Organizational Culture and Leadership* (San Francisco, CA: Jossey-Bass, 2010).

Chapter One: Getting a Vision

1. "The Habit of Making Value," https://www.youtube.com/watch?v=y-e0lQ-dYmQ (accessed January 14, 2019).
2. Evangelism is Most Effective among Kids," Barna Group, https://www.barna.com/research/evangelism-is-most-effective-among-kids/ (accessed January 14, 2019).
3. Real Life Church, http://www.reallifechurchrva.org
4. Barna, *Reviving Evangelism* (n.p.: Barna Group, 2019), 9.
5. https://www.madetoflourish.org/
6. https://university.acton.org/
7. https://churchmultiplication.net/
8. https://www.mosaix2019.com/our-speakers/

Chapter Two: What is a Church for Monday?

1. Gea Gort and Mats Tunehag, *BAM Global Movement: Business as mission concept & stories* (Peabody, MA: HndricksonPublishers, 2018), 89.
2. "Top Voting Issues in 2016 Election," Pew Research Center, July 7, 2016, https://www.people-press.org/2016/07/07/4-top-voting-issues-in-2016-election (accessed May 13, 2019).
3. Gabriella Bradford Sr. Manager, Performance Marketing at Bliss, Los Angeles, CA.
4. Christianity Today, https://www.christianitytoday.com/edstetzer/2019/june/8-

simple-rules-for-movement-part-6-co-vocational.html(accessed July 10 2019)

Chapter Three: Chart the Path Forward

1. https://www.madetoflourish.org
2. https://www.theologyofwork.org

Chapter Four: Context, Content, and Consequences of a Post-Modern, Post-Christian, and Post Truth Society

1. Robert Webber, *Who Gets to Narrate the World? Contending for the Christian Story in an Age of Rivals* (Downers Grove, IL: IVP Books, 2008), 90; citing Robert Webber and Phil Kenyon "A Call to an Ancient Evangelical Future" (Northern Seminary, 2006).
2. Grenz, 43; quoting Hugh Tomlinson, *"After Truth: Post-Modernism and the Rhetoric of Science,"* in Institute of Contemporary Arts (London, England), Hilary Lawson and Lisa Appignanesi, *Dismantling Truth: Reality in the Post-Modern World* (New York: St. Martin's Press, 1989), 12-17.
3. Ibid., 16-17.
4. Rene Pache, *The Inspiration and Authority of Scripture*, trans. Helen Needham (Chicago: Moody, 1969), 313.
5. Barna Group, *Barna Trends 2018: The Truth about a Post-truth Society* (Grand Rapids, MI: Baker Books, 2017), 116- 117.
6. Mark Liederbach and Alvin L. Reid, *The Convergent Church: Missional Worshipers in an Emerging Culture* (Grand Rapids, MI: Kregel Publications, 2009), 59-60.
7. Ibid., 23.
8. Liederback, 59.
9. Millard Erickson, *Postmodernizing the Faith: Evangelical Responses to the Challenge of Postmodernism* (Grand Rapids, MI: Baker Books, 1998), 19.
10. Barna Group, "Americans Are Most Likely to Base Truth on Feelings," http://www.barna.org/ barna-update/article/5-barna-update/67-americans-are-most-likely-to-base-truth-on-feelings (accessed April 25, 2019).
11. Ibid.

12. Barna Group, *Barna Trends* 2018, 117.
13. Ibid.
14. Grenz, 14-15.
15. Charles Colson and Nancy Pearcey, *How Now Shall We Live?* (Wheaton, IL: Tyndale House Publishers, 1999), 23
16. Grenz, 14.
17. Erickson,19.
18. Walt Anderson, *Reality Isn't What It Used to Be: Theatrical Politics, Ready-to-Wear Religion, Global Myths, Primitive Chic, and Other Wonders of the Postmodern World* (San Francisco, CA: HarperSanFrancisco, 1992), 183.
19. Grenz, 55.
20. Liederbach, 59; see also D. A. Carson, *The Intolerance of Tolearance* (Grand Rapids, MI: Eerdmans, 2012).
21. Colson, 23.
22. Barna Group, "Americans Are Most Likely to Base Truth on Feelings."
23. Ibid.
24. Bill Reinhold, "What is the Missional Church? A Brief Introduction," Church Innovations, http://www.churchinnovations.org/02_missional/mc_main.htm l (accessed April 5, 2012).
25. Pew Research Center, "When Americans Say They Believe in God, What Do They Mean?," https://www.pewforum.org/2018/04/25/when-americans-say-they-believe-in-god-what-do-they-mean (accessed April 25, 2019).
26. James A. Herrick, *The Making of a New Spirituality: the Eclipse of the Western Religoius Tradition* (Downers Grove, IL: IntervarsityPress, 2003, 277.
27. Frank Newport, "One-Third of Americans Believe the Bible Is Literally True: High Inverse Correlation Between Education and Belief in a Literal Bible," Gallup News Service, http://www.gallup.com/poll/27682/onethird-americans-believe-bible-literally-true.aspx (accessed May 25, 2012).
28. Barna Group, "Most American Christians Do Not Believe that Satan or the Holy Spirit Exist," Barna.org, https://www.barna.com/research/most-american-christians-

do-not-believe-that-satan-or-the-holy-spirit-exist/ (accessed April 25, 2019).

29. Barna Group, "Americans Are Most Likely to Base Truth on Feelings."

Chapter Five: What are the Spiritual Currents in Western Culture?

1. Barna, *Reviving Evangelism* (n.p.: Barna Group, 2019), 19.
2. Stanley J.Grenz, *Primer on Postmodernism* (Grand Rapids, MI: William B. Eerdmans, 1996), 39.
3. Ibid.,40.
4. Webber, 11.
5. Derrell Guder, *The Continuing Conversion of the Church* (Grand Rapids, MI: Eerdmans Publishing, 2000), 102.
6. Webber, 137.
7. Ibid., 137.
8. Ibid., 76.
9. Ibid., 77.
10. Ibid., 75-76.
11. Amy Sherman, *Kingdom Calling: Vocational Stewardship for the Common Good* (Downers Grove, IL: InterVarsity Press, 2011), Kindle e-book, locations 681-83.
12. Ibid., locations 718-25; citing Dallas Willard, *The Great Omission: Reclaiming Jesus' Essential Teaching on Discipleship* (New York: HarperOne, 2006), 4.
13. Cheryl Bridges Johns, "Theological Challenges of the Spirit-empowered Church in the United States" (paper presented at the joint meeting of the Society of Pentecostal Studies and Empowered 21, Virginia Beach, VA, March 1, 2012).
14. George G. Hunter III, *The Apostolic Congregation: Church Growth Reconceived for a New Generation* (Nashville, TN: Abingdon Press, 2009), Kindle e-book, locations 386-88.
15. Ibid., locations 391-92.
16. Herrick, 17.
17. Ibid., 18.
18. Ibid., 37-38.
19. Guder, 117.
20. Ibid., 120.

21. Christopher J. H. Wright, *The Mission of God: Unlocking the Bible's Grand Narrative* (Downers Grove, IL: IVP Academic, 2008), 22-23.

Chapter Six: On Mission with God is a Twenty-First Century World

1. "10 Facts about America's Churchless," Barna Group, https://www.barna.com/research/10-facts-about-americas-churchless (accessed May 21, 2019).
2. Ibid.
3. Colson, 22.
4. Barna, *Reviving Evangelism* (n.p.: Barna Group, 2019), 21.
5. Vinay Samuel and Chris Sugden, *Mission as Transformation: A Theology of the Whole Gospel* (Carlisle, CA: Paternoster Publishing, 1999), 179.
6. Derrell Guder, *The Continuing Conversion of the Church* (Grand Rapids, MI: Eerdmans Publishing, 2000), 68.
7. Tom Nelson, *The Economics of Neighborly Love* (Downers Grove, IL: InterVarsity Press, 2017), 5.
8. Clark H. Pinnock, "The Holy Spirit as a Distinct Person in the Godhead," in *Spirit and Renewal: Essays in Honor of J. Rodman Williams*, ed. Mark W. Wilson, 34–41, (Grand Rapids, MI: Zondervan, 1994), 39.
9. Abraham Kuyper, *Wisdom and Wonder: Common Grace in Science and Art* (Grand Rapids, MI: Christian's Library Press, 2011), Kindle e-book, locations 629–31.
10. S. L. Cox and K. H. Easley, *Holman Christian Standard Bible: Harmony of the Gospels* (Nashville, TN: Holman Bible Publishers, 2007), 345.
11. Christopher J. H. Wright, *The Mission of God: Unlocking the Bible's Grand Narrative* (Downers Grove, IL: IVP Academic, 2008), 221.
12. Ibid., 214.
13. Ibid., 221.
14. Christopher J. H. Wright, *The Mission of God's People: A Biblical Theology of the Church's Mission* (Grand Rapids, MI: Zondervan, 2010), Kindle e-book, locations 173–75.

15. Greek, *apostellō*, cf. "apostle." *Blue Letter Bible*, https://www.blueletterbible.org/lang/lexicon/lexicon.cfm?Strongs=G649&t=KJV (accessed March 28, 2019).
16. Wright, *The Mission of God*, 243.
17. All Scripture references, unless otherwise noted, are from the New International Version, 1984.
18. "*Apollymi*: Strong's G622," Blue Letter Bible, http://www.blueletterbible.org/lang/lexicon/lexicon.cfm?Strongs=G622&t=KJV (accessed May 11, 2019).
19. Mark Deymaz, *Disruption* (Nashville, TN: Harper Collins, 2017), 84.
20. Ibid., 111.
21. Ibid., 79.
22. Ibid., 85–86.
23. Ibid., 93–94.
24. Deymaz, *Disruption*, 93.
25. Ibid., 92.

Chapter Seven: Outside the Church Walls

1. References in this book to the apostolic take into consideration this traditional understanding of the word (Robert J. Scudieri, *The Apostolic Church: One, Holy, Catholic and Missionary* [Chino, CA: Lutheran Society for Missiology, 1995], 13).
2. David Clark, "Ephesians 4:7–16: The Pauline Perspective of Pentecost," in *Faces of Renewal: Studies in Honor of Stanley M. Horton*, ed. Paul Elbert, 128–35, (Eugene, OR: Wipf & Stock, 1988), 129.
3. Ibid., 132.
4. Robert Menzies, *Empowered for Witness: The Spirit in Luke-Acts* (Sheffield, UK: Sheffield Academic Press, 1994), 257.
5. David Lim, *Spiritual Gifts: A Fresh Look* (Springfield, MO: Gospel Publishing House, 1991), 45.
6. Clark, 134–35.
7. Barna, "Church Attendance Trends Around the Country," May 26, 2017, https://www.barna.com/research/church-attendance-trends-around-country (accessed, May, 20, 2019).
8. Barna, *Christians at Work* (n.p.: Barna Group, 2019), 21.
9. Ibid., 48–49.

10. Ibid., 67.
11. Ibid, 58–64.
12. Guy P. Duffield and Nathaniel M. Van Cleave, *Foundations of Pentecostal Theology* (Los Angeles, CA: L.I.F.E. Bible College, 1983), 443–44.
13. Barna, *Christians at Work*, 50.
14. Barna, *Christians at Work*, 93, 94.
15. Barna, *Christians at Work*, 50.
16. Barna, *Christians at Work*, 96, 97.
17. Wright, *The Mission of God's People*, locations 3272–74.
18. Robert J. Scudieri, *The Apostolic Church: One, Holy, Catholic and Missionary* (Chino, CA: Lutheran Society for Missiology, 1995), 78–79.
19. Wright, *The Mission of God's People*, locations 606–8.
20. Parts of this story are adapted from Luke Bobo, "The Sermon That Changed This Immigrant's Life: From Jobless to Business Owner," Made to Flourish, November 2, 2017, https://www.madetoflourish.org/resources/jobless-to-business-owner/.

Chapter Eight: Invested in Cultural Transformation

1. Schein, 32.
2. Gordon D. Fee, *Paul, the Spirit, and the People of God* (Peabody, MA: Hendrickson Publishers, 1996), 66.
3. Chris Jehle, "A Practitioner's Case for Theological Engagement," Christian Community Development Association (*CCDA Theological Journal 2012*), 41, http://ccda.uberflip.com/i/82984 (accessed May 12,2019)
4. Ed Silvoso, *Anointed for Business* (Ventura, CA: Regal Books, 2002), 18.
5. At the Kingdom's full consummation, all cultures will be God fearing: "every knee will bow before me; and every tongue will confess to God" (Rom. 14:11); also see: Isaiah 45:23; Philippians 2:10.
6. A comprehensive demographic study of more than 200 countries finds that there are 2.18 billion Christians of all ages around the world, representing nearly a third of the estimated 2010 global population of 6.9 billion. For details on this data see

Pew Forum on Religion and Public Life, "A Report on the Size and Distribution of the World's Christian Population," Pew Forum, http://www.pewforum.org/Christian/Global-Christianity-exec.aspx (accessed May 20, 2019).

Chapter Nine: Scorecard

1. W. E. H. Lecky, *History of European Morals from Augustus to Charlemagne*, 3rd. rev. ed. (New York: Appleton, 1916), 338.
2. Umidi, Joseph, *Transformational Coaching: Bridge Building that Impacts, Connects, and Advances the Ministry and the Marketplace* (Fairfax,VA: Xulon Press, 2005), 195.
3. McNeal, Reggie. "3 Epic Shifts Underway in the Church" filmed 2019. YouTube Video, 4:13. Posted 2019. https://youtu.be/MT54Q73dnD4 (accessed June 27 2019)
4. Neil Patel, "90% of Startups Fail: Here's What You Need to Know About the 10%," Forbes.com, Jan. 16, 2015. http://www.forbes.com/sites/neilpatel/2015/01/16/90-of-startups-will-fail-heres-what-you-need-to-know-about-the-10/#4d5d7cbe55e1 (accessed July 11 2019).

Chapter Ten: Recovering Relevance: Practitioners and Thought Leaders on Being a Church for Monday

1. Made to Flourish, https://www.madetoflourish.org/
2. Jim Clifton, The Coming Jobs War (New York: Gallup Press, 2011), 10.
3. *The Economics of Neighborly Love* by Tom Nelson. Copyright (c) 2017 by Tom Nelson. Used by permission of InterVarsity Press, P.O. Box 1400, Downers Grove, IL 60515, USA. www.ivpress.com
4. Steve Pike is President and Founder of Urban Islands Project, and author, and co-author of several books— *Leading Church Multiplication, Total Fitness For Your Church*, and his forthcoming one, *City: How to Increase the Presence of the Church in the City Near You*. Steve's passion for church multiplication began in 1989 when Steve and his wife, Cherri, pioneered a new church that became the catalyst of a church

planting movement in the state of Utah that continues to this day. The Pikes make their home in Denver, Colorado.

5. Senator Amanda Chase began serving in the Virginia State Senate in 2016. She grew up in Chesterfield County, graduated from Virginia Tech and married her high school sweetheart. They have been married for more than twenty-seven years and have four grown children. Chase has served in management in the banking and credit finance industry in both the public and private sector. For more than three years she hosted a radio talk show Cut to the Chase with Senator Chase on WNTW 820AM.

6. Chuck Proudfit embodies the term "co-vocational." He came to Christ as a young adult, shortly after founding a business consultancy called SKILLSOURCE, which he continues to lead. In addition, Chuck is the founder and President of At Work on Purpose, a citywide workplace ministry with over 10,000 members in Cincinnati, Ohio, USA. Chuck is also an ordained pastor, a marketplace minister at Grace Chapel in Mason, Ohio; an Executive Board Member for Self Sustaining Enterprises; and a City Network Leader for Made to Flourish.

7. Leah Archibald spent a decade in high–tech marketing while earning an MBA from Babson College. Today she writes for the Theology of Work Project where she connects the Bible to work that Christians do every day. Leah's devotionals on topics such as Anxiety About Money and How to Make the Right Decision have been completed online by over 500,000 Christians.

8. Karley Hatter has an MA in Theology and Ministry from Fuller Theological Seminary. She works at Fuller De Pree Center as Network and Collaboration Manager. Karley has also started her brand, She Co. that equips women who are seeking to grow in their vocations and understanding of God and his work in the world. Karley is a preacher, networker, and coffee connoisseur.

9. David Kinnaman is president of The Barna Group, which provides research and resources that facilitate spiritual transformation in people's lives. Since joining Barna in 1995, Kinnaman has designed and analyzed nearly five hundred studies for a variety of churches, nonprofits, and corporations. This essay is an excerpt from Barna's study of teens thirteen- to

eighteen-years old, *Gen Z: The Culture, Beliefs and Motivations Shaping the Next Generation* (Barna, 2017) and *Making Gen Z Disciples* by David Kinnaman and Barna Group (Barna, [January, 23, 2018]), and is given to the author as contribution to this book.

10. Cassandra Ferguson has twenty-five years as a ministry leader and business owner, and more recently her own radio talk show. Ferguson is a certified organization and business strategist through Villanova University and spends her weeks in inner city schools as a program manager with a non-profit organization teaching young people about financial literacy.

11. Linda Evans Shepherd is a best-selling, Selah-award-winning author of more than thirty-five books including *When You Don't Know What to Pray* and her latest, *When You Need to Move a Mountain*. She is an internationally recognized speaker and is the president of Right to the Heart Ministries and the CEO of the Advanced Writers and Speakers Association (AWSA.) She's both the publisher of *Leading Hearts Magazine*, a multiple EPA-award winning magazine for Christian women leaders and "Arise Daily," a daily e-devotional.

12. All quotations in this contribution are from the NIV.

13. Abraham Kuyper, *Abraham Kuyper: A Centennial Reader*, ed. James D. Bratt (Grand Rapids, Michigan: William B. Eerdmans, 1998), 488.

14. Rev. Dr. Mark D. Roberts is Executive Director of Fuller's Max De Pree Center for Leadership. A parish pastor for twenty-five years and a non-profit leader for twelve, Mark is committed to the integration of faith, work, and economic wisdom for the flourishing of the church and world. An author of eight books, most recently a commentary on Ephesians (Story of God series), Mark is the principal writer of "Life for Leaders," the De Pree Center's daily email devotional.

15. Tom Thatcher serves as Professor of Biblical Studies and Provost at Cincinnati Christian University. Thatcher is the author/editor of twenty books on the New Testament and Christian Origins, with a particular interest in the Johannine Literature and early Christian media culture. For the past six years, he has served as the VP of Academic Affairs of his school,

with oversight of all academic and student life programming. Tom is also an ordained minister and a founding partner of Elemental Churches consulting (www.elementalchurches.com).

About the Author

Dr. Svetlana Papazov is a wife, mother of two, lead pastor, educator, and entrepreneur. She is the President of Real Life Center for Entrepreneurial and Leadership Excellence in Richmond, Virginia and President Elect of National Speakers Association Virginia. Svetlana speaks nationwide at Acton University, Made to Flourish Common Good Conference, Mosaix and various denominational and church events. Additionally, she has been featured in and written for well-known publications and magazines such as Barna: The State of Pastors, Influence magazine, Evangel, Enrichment Journal, and more.

Svetlana loves creativity in all its forms, enjoys the beauty of water color art, and treasures her solitude with God before plunging into her daily schedule. She guards with passion the time for the after-work walks with her husband Michael where they often dream the futures the Holy Spirit stirs in their hearts.

What excites Svetlana the most is unleashing human potential and having a front row seat in the development of influencers. That is why she has transitioned from a life of a business owner of multiple enterprises to a life of an equipper of leaders. She speaks at, consults, and trains various denominational networks, associations, churches, and marketplace leaders to become transformation catalysts for their communities.

If you enjoyed Church for Monday and would like to resource yourself further by booking Svetlana for speaking, consulting, or training contact her at: www.SvetlanaPapazov.com

Before You Go...

Share your thoughts with your friends

- Share on Facebook, Instagram, or Tweeter that you finished Church for Monday
- Write a Review on Amazon.com, CBD.com, Walmart.com
- Blog: Subscribe to churchformonday.com for Svetlana's blog, news and updates
- YouTube: Subscribe to Svetlana's YouTube Chanel at www.reallifechurchrva.org/media
- Facebook: Like "Church for Monday" on Facebook
- LinkedIn: Connect with Svetlana on LinkedIn @Svetlana Papazov, Dr.
- Instagram: Connect with Svetlana on Instagram @svetlana.papazov
- Tweeter: Follow her on Tweeter @SvetlanaPapazov
- Learn about Svetlana's ministries and speaking schedule at www.SvetlanaPapazov.com